T0169633

marketing masters

What Others are Saying...

Connie's one-on-one coaching has been invaluable in getting my business off the ground. Business planning and marketing are second nature to this pro, she thinks of everything! Connie feels like my partner and to a new entrepreneur, this is very comforting. She gives so much of herself, is very supportive and has an amazing interest in my success. Thank you Connie, I couldn't have done it without you.

—**Virginia Becker**, Entrepreneur
electronic pet assistance directory (e-p.a.d)

When Connie Pheiff speaks, her audience listens and learns! Connie was a popular speaker at the Called Woman Conference 2013, and what a story she has to share. It is the best kind of story of all—one with a surprise ending that will encourage and inspire you to discover your calling, overcome obstacles and live with passion. Connie's presentation sparkles and shines with her wit and powerful story. She is going to change your life!

—**Lynne Watts**, President/CEO, The Called Woman Conference

Connie translates the value of organizational effectiveness, inspires, and encourages others to define their personal success equation. Connie enlists support from others to accomplish individual and team goals. She strives to improve the values, behaviors, standards, and practices reflective of the entrepreneur's vision and adapts leadership style to a variety of situations. Connie empowers tomorrow's workforce.

—**Matthew Turowski, Esq.** , Rosenn Jenkins Greenwald, LLP

Connie presented at the Foundation Center, Cleveland. She is an inspiration and thought leader. I learned a great deal from her to implement in my business.

—**Megan Quinn**, Development Officer, The MetroHealth System

Connie has demonstrated impressive organizational skills. We raised over $100,000 in one week and brought in new members and couldn't have done it without her help. Throughout my travels, often the first comment made is one complimenting Connie's talents and professionalism.

—**Lonnie Taylor**, Senior Vice President,
U.S. Chamber of Commerce

Connie is dynamic…facilitating workshops for American Red Cross Chapter Leadership that was engaging, thought provoking, and inspiring! Connie's expert knowledge provided answers and a call to action...her preparation, program, leadership, and pleasing personality! A+++++

—**Cindy Garren**, Major Gifts Officer, American Red Cross

Connie delivered a flawless presentation to our Chamber business membership full of wit and wisdom with an entertaining twist. I highly recommend her presentation when you are looking to inspire all audiences.

—**Mari Potis**, VP Events,
Greater Scranton Chamber of Commerce

Thank you, Connie. You led a really fabulous presentation. On their way out, many women were chatting about the tools and resources you provided…they were very enthusiastic going forward. Job well done!

—**Brynne Zaniboni**, Dress for Success Worldwide-West

marketing masters

Ready, Set, GROW Your Market

CONNIE PHEIFF

NEW YORK

marketing masters
Ready, Set, GROW Your Market

© 2015 CONNIE PHEIFF.

All rights reserved. No portion of this book may be reproduced, stored in a retrieval system, or transmitted in any form or by any means—electronic, mechanical, photocopy, recording, scanning, or other,—except for brief quotations in critical reviews or articles, without the prior written permission of the publisher.

Published in New York, New York, by Morgan James Publishing. Morgan James and The Entrepreneurial Publisher are trademarks of Morgan James, LLC.
www.MorganJamesPublishing.com

The Morgan James Speakers Group can bring authors to your live event. For more information or to book an event visit The Morgan James Speakers Group at www.TheMorganJamesSpeakersGroup.com.

A **free** eBook edition is available with the purchase of this print book.

ISBN 978-1-63047-397-6 paperback
ISBN 978-1-63047-398-3 eBook
ISBN 978-1-63047-399-0 hardcover
Library of Congress Control Number:
2014948650

CLEARLY PRINT YOUR NAME ABOVE IN UPPER CASE

Instructions to claim your free eBook edition:
1. Download the BitLit app for Android or iOS
2. Write your name in **UPPER CASE** on the line
3. Use the BitLit app to submit a photo
4. Download your eBook to any device

Cover Design by:
Rachel Lopez
www.r2cdesign.com

Interior Design by:
Bonnie Bushman
bonnie@caboodlegraphics.com

In an effort to support local communities, raise awareness and funds, Morgan James Publishing donates a percentage of all book sales for the life of each book to Habitat for Humanity Peninsula and Greater Williamsburg.

Get involved today, visit
www.MorganJamesBuilds.com

Habitat for Humanity
Peninsula and
Greater Williamsburg
Building Partner

also by CONNIE PHEIFF

The Art of the Ask
Get into your fundraising groove

The Art of the Ask
A collection of fundraising letters and telephone scripts

Coaching Program by Connie Pheiff
Green Apples Impact Academy

Radio Program by Connie Pheiff
Marketing Masters
Innovate + Captivate = Convert

Meet Connie online and receive free training at
www.conniepheiffspeaks.com

**In an effort to support local communities, raise awareness and
funds. Connie Pheiff Speaks, Inc. donates one percent of all book
sales for the life of each book to Dress for Success. Get involved
today, visit www.dressforsuccess.org**

DEDICATED to my husband for helping me
to recognize anything is possible.

To my children: be yourself — be honest — do your best

table of contents

author's note

I am a recovering executive and successfully transformed to the title of 'entrepreneur.' But lets not use titles. I wrote this book to help business leaders transform their organization and/or transform their passion into a profession. The tools found in this book can be successfully implemented by entrepreneurs, Fortune 500 CEO's, sales teams, and nonprofit executives. The business environment is constantly ravaged with changes — *Marketing Masters* provides creative strategies colliding the old school of marketing with today's digital strategies connecting with the NOW generation. You will immediately convert consumers to customers, relationships into partnerships, and ideas into realities.

Marketing Masters is actually quite simple, its how you…

INNOVATE — CAPTIVATE = CONVERT

INNOVATE – Make a change in something already established

CAPTIVATE – Attract and hold the interest and attention of your potential customer

CONVERT – To persuade a consumer to become your loyal customer

The teachings and stories in this book can be read from different perspectives: entrepreneurs, Fortune 500 CEO's, sales teams, and nonprofit executives.

Whether your organization is large or small, this book gives you the tools to determine if you are using smart marketing strategies. In the end, all business leaders should consider implementing the old school of marketing and creating a global presence on social media networks. Your customer needs to know, like, and respect you. And know that you serve them.

Here's a model I often use. I refer to this model as creative marketing.

- 40% of my time is building rapport and trust
- 30% of my time is identifying customer needs
- 20% of my time is product knowledge
- 10% of my time is gaining customer commitment

This model shared with me by my Business Coach, Dan Miller, can be used for creating your business action plans and marketing your services.

Unfortunately, organizations are looking at the economies of scale and cutting their traditional marketing efforts. If your current marketing efforts are not working, I can bet money it's your marketing strategies.

Today's consumer is smarter; they take longer to evaluate what you are offering. They have immediate access to the World Wide Web where they will immediately say positive or negative feedback about you.

I hear the same from nonprofit organizations. Giving is decreasing. I assure you that Philanthropic giving is not disappearing. Giving simply looks different these days, and we need to be open to the ways of work. With change come new opportunities. The big change we're realizing is that the world is much more flat and connected than we ever thought possible. This means you have greater opportunities to increase your business value.

Are you in the right business? You may have a passion for your enterprise, but do you have what it takes to "ask" for the sale? My coach has taught me that 85% of success is having confidence from looking within. It's time for you to take that look within yourself.

Get ready to be blown away. This will only happen if you're ready and have an open mind to change. I'll focus on colliding old school marketing with today's digital trends, the importance of service, not sales, and proposals that can be easily and quickly modified for an entrepreneur looking to secure corporate partners.

Here is your first eye opener; many believe nonprofit organizations alone have the benefit of securing corporate sponsorships. WRONG! When you're watching your next NASCAR race take notice of the sponsors. NASCAR is not a nonprofit organization. They are for profit.

*"Remember the words of the Lord Jesus, how he said,
'It is more blessed to give than to receive.'"*
—**Acts 20:35**

*"We make a living by what we get,
but we make a life by what we give."*
—**Winston Churchill**

*"In the long run, we shape our lives, and we shape
ourselves. The process never ends until we die. And the
choices we make are ultimately our own responsibility."*
—**Eleanor Roosevelt**

"A dream is a reality waiting for you to get there."
—**Connie Pheiff**

foreword

We've seen Jeff Skoll (eBay), Mark Zuckerberg (Facebook), Bill Gates (Microsoft), Warren Buffet (Berkshire Hathaway), Michael Bloomberg (New York City mayor and founder of Bloomberg financial news service), and others commit to The Giving Pledge—pledging to give away at least half of their wealth to philanthropic causes. These individuals built for-profit businesses but then structured those profits to be plowed into worthy endeavors.

However, the key concept in understanding how to tap into these rich resources is not to simply raise your hand as a start-up business. These wealthy entrepreneurs are looking far beyond just the legal structure to the very things that allowed their businesses to be so successful. In the for-profit world, poor financial controls, inability to adapt, fierce competition, ineffective management, technology and social media changes cause businesses to close or be swallowed by similar organizations. Knowledgeable business leaders are quick to recognize similar challenges in small to mid-size businesses.

Innovative types of organizations are blurring the distinctions between corporate and entrepreneurial entities. New terms like social entrepreneurship, ethical capitalism and "B" corporations are emerging and showing their ability to address issues like pollution, poverty and illiteracy that were historically only the domain of the public sector. John Sage (Pura Vida Coffee), Tom Szaky (TerraCycle), Blake Mycoskie (TOMS Shoes) and many others are leading the way with business models that are doing well while doing good. In today's economic workplace you can change the world, address poverty or pollution, make the world a better place—*and make money* in the process.

Bottom line: The legal structure of an organization is less important than having a worthy mission to fulfill—and a business structure that is efficient and compelling. Success in business requires a clear understanding of the principles you will see in this book.

As clarified in **Marketing Masters** creative marketing for entrepreneurs is much like effective marketing in any business. Ultimately customer's give to people they know, like and trust. You are selling an idea, a cause, a better way of life or a solution to a recognized problem. In the world of selling we often tell people that true, professional selling is simply sharing enthusiasm. But as Connie advocates you need to serve, not sell.

To compete in today's marketplace we have to compete on quality and value to earn the right to ask people to support our enterprise. We can't offer shoddy service, inefficient money management, shoddy necklaces or second-rate coffee and expect people to get excited about helping us in our worthy endeavors. We have to believe we are the very best. We have to be proud of what we are representing and then hold our heads high as we invite people to be part of something great.

Our passion for what we are doing can then exceed any fear or sense of inadequacy.

You are reading a tool that will enhance your ability to do something great. *Marketing Masters* provides the steps to standing above the crowd. You deserve more than just adequate resources. You can tap into the rich resources of wealth waiting to purchase your service and products.

Being excellent at serving your customers - making profits - requires more than having a passion. *Marketing Masters* can put you in the top 5% of entrepreneurial experts, or the top 5% in business profitability. This success, as in any area of life, is not luck. Rather, it's when preparation meets opportunity. Enjoy your *preparation.*

—**Dan Miller**, coach and author (*48 Days to the Work You Love*)

introduction

You can do a simple Internet search and find many "how-to's" for marketing your business. What's missing? It's simple creative marketing for entrepreneurs. Many suggest the only thing that really matters is that you have a great product for your customers. For the last 12 years I've spent my time as an international speaker, traveling the world talking about creative marketing. I'm also an executive coach. I get a chance to meet lots of great entrepreneurs. I always get the same question "how do I market without breaking the bank?"

I began my career working in the nonprofit sector with little or no budget for marketing. My first position with the United States Chamber of Commerce was selling membership. From there I moved into a Director position with a local Chamber of Commerce where I was thrown into the fire to create a member benefit that would increase membership. The growth of the program I developed was incredible. Bank presidents were fighting to become a member. When I became the Chief Executive Officer of the Girl Scouts my brand was so strong that our girl membership increased by 86% in my first year.

Building a strong brand is important to build your business. However, I believe we need to go deeper. Ask yourself, "What do we want to project about our business." You need to build capacity for change then you can get clarity of how to effectively market your business with creativity without breaking the bank. We loose clarity sometimes because we get too busy putting out the daily fires. Continue reading and you will learn my unique system of creative marketing strategies for building customer loyalty.

How do you stand out and get noticed?

Marketing Masters is learning how to serve your customers, not sell.

I'm not going to talk about the historical philosophies that surround selling products. If you are like me, you have already listened to motivational CDs, read inspirational books, and attended seminars to learn how to increase your motivation to sell. In plain language I will provide examples of real world experiences and what I recommend as the most valuable pieces of information you need to be a successful marketer for your business.

My best creative marketing efforts were with the United States Chamber of Commerce. My work was directly with the president of the Chamber and the senior vice presidents. Initially, I started as a telephone sales representative. (Hey, we all have to start somewhere, right?) I was quickly promoted to downtown Washington D.C., right across from the White House. I had made it! I was working in the District! Honestly, this was one of the best times of my professional career.

My position was to work with the executive team to develop a 16-month plan to revitalize the United States Chamber of Commerce. Here are the highlights:

1. Fix the infrastructure through finances and membership recruitment, and put retention systems in place.
2. Reorganize the membership system.
3. Enhance the commercial operations and partnerships.
4. Strengthen relationships of state and local Chambers of Commerce, government officials, and the media.
5. Advance the core agenda.
6. Defend businesses against attacks on the enterprise system.

Funding in large amounts needed to happen for these changes to take place. For nearly 18 months, a 40-city tour took place; we visited corridors of power in Washington, D.C., and across the country asking for BIG money.

We learn from our experiences and this experience taught me that we must serve our customers before we can make a sale. This program was successful because the Chamber first and foremost provided a service to its members. Once the members seen the benefit, they were open to supporting the organization.

I continue to follow the same philosophy for my business. I provide a service to my clients by following digital trends, offering advice, promoting my usefulness for my customers, having a great organization, considerate and easy to work with, and being the easiest speaker an event has ever worked with. This is my promise.

Of course, these are just two examples of my business success. In this book I will share best practices—ones I learned from my mentors as well as the ones I gleaned from the school of hard knocks. You'll learn how your skills and experiences are not good enough. You need to stand out and be different than competition. I will share hands-on strategies that will make your marketing efforts more prosperous. Without going broke.

You're an entrepreneur. Ask yourself are you all in or just have a toe in the water. This book is not meant to simplify your existence, choosing to be a successful business owner takes hard work. I am here to streamline your efforts. Refer to these pages time and time again, and you'll soon join the list of entrepreneurs who choose to become **Marketing Masters.**

how i got here...
lemons to lemonade

the excitement as the Chief Executive Officer for a nonprofit organization came to a screeching halt in June 2006. It wasn't the first time of disappointment in my life, and certainly not the last. Accepting the CEO position for the Girl Scouts was one of the greatest moments in my professional career. Or so I thought. When I heard the words "you are no longer an employee of the organization" my heart sunk. What would I do now? I didn't have plan B. Like many others, I assumed employment with this organization was until retirement. I ass-u-me wrong!

I knew the completion of the realignment was just around the corner. For 12 months—365 days I embraced the task of creating a high-capacity organization for Northeast Pennsylvania. Hundreds of volunteers and staff would come together for many hours deliberating and designing a new business model that consists of best practices. The new business model was easily approved by the board of directors to pave the way for the new leadership to implement.

For me, becoming part of the new leadership team was not to be. I applied for the new Chief Executive Officer position. I wanted to lead the new council so desperately that I hired a resume writer and interview coach. None-the-less, the position was not to be mine.

For months to follow I became depressed and emotionally dead. Didn't know where to turn. I was applying to nearly every Girl Scout CEO available position from Maine to Miami. No one wanted me. I was rejected over and over again. My health started to fail and I finally decided I had to turn attitude around. I went back to school and finished with a double Masters in Public Administration and Organizational Innovation with a minor in speech and marketing. I immersed myself in something I could control escaping from my problems and depression.

Now here I was with a degree in hand. During my educational years I would consult with executives helping them to understand the importance of creating a high-capacity organizations. Each time fundraising came to the table and ways to market without breaking the bank. Before long I was creating a system of creative marketing strategies for nonprofit organizations. It occurred to me my greatest moment in my career were not only fundraising, like I did with the United States Chamber of Commerce, it was how I was able to develop creative market strategies.

The light bulb went off, perhaps you're a recovering executive like me, when I realized my system of creative marketing strategies not only apply to nonprofit organizations, they also apply to an entrepreneurial business - a system that I employ in my business each day - a system that I want to share with you.

As a business leader, you're challenged of the "how to's" for marketing to your customer, or want to re-vitalize your current marketing strategies without breaking the bank. Look no further, I'll provide you a time-tested system with real-world examples of old and new creative marketing strategies as we focus on digital trends.

define
creative marketing

ccording to the American Marketing Association (AMA, 2014) marketing is the activity, set of institutions, and processes for creating, communicating, delivering, and exchanging offerings that have value for customers, clients, partners, and society at large.

Traditionally, marketing consisted mostly of advertising in magazines, newspapers, television, and radio and lets not forget the dreaded billboards. Advertisements typically are designed to meet the standards of the ad size for the medium and corresponding material.

When I started marketing for the nonprofit sector or asking for donations to support a favorite nonprofit happened by hanging out on the street corner or going door-to-door, such as selling Girl Scout cookies. These days, marketing takes on many forms as social networking is emerging and supports your grassroots marketing efforts. From a direct "ask" for money to events and product sales, marketing needs to be a constant allowing you to achieve your business goals.

Remember those good ole' days of marketing? Billboards, high-priced television advertising, and lets not forget cold calling. Fast-forward to today's virtual marketing, which changes rapidly. Not long ago, like 2 seconds ago, email was the latest platform for media. Change is sharp; it brings a wide list of choices to communicate with customers, from SMS to social networking, to white papers. How do you keep track of it all? Which is the best platform for your business?

Marketing Masters provides tools to help you do more with less, while driving results you can measure through our three-part platform, C.S.!. and see immediate transformational results.

CHANGE – define the problem and make a decision to change your marketing system. Use a blend of the traditional approach with a large dose of breaking the rules.

SUSTAIN – when you deliver relevant content and serve your audience, not sell. I believe in evolution, not revolution. Marketing is a process, taking the best of what works, eliminating what doesn't work, and keeping your eye on what is possible.

!NNOVATE – Simplify your interaction with your marketplace by creating a system that simplifies your approach. Add an infusion of technology, and you create an innovative dynamic new way to build your brand, create awareness, and drive sales.

Creative marketing is going beyond the norm. It's a brave new world of marketing. The new normal requires a new type of thinking.

Why is Creative Marketing Important?

As an entrepreneurial business leader, creative marketing is a key skill to drive business results. Marketing is creativity, foundation, design, integrated, purpose, promotion, profit, and strategic. Getting the word out about your business needs to be constant. It's become more challenging in today's noisy marketplace, but not impossible when you create a system that is intentional and constant, without breaking the bank. If you want to stay in the game and win your marketing must be so captivating, it can't be ignored.

Here are five bold creative marketing moves from entrepreneurs. This is a mix of business size, revenue large and small. (Linkner, J. 2013)

Dove: The Company dared to be different by showing real women and their bodies in all their ads. Changing from the rail-thin models with heavy photo-enhancing beauties, Dove exposed this hypocrisy to the world. This change was an evolution allowing women to feel better about them—and buy Dove products because of how they've were impacted by the creative marketing strategy.

Cuties: The mandarin orange, aka clementine, is an orange. The difference is how Cuties is marketing this brand to its customer. They are marketing to children with its campaign that "Kids love Cuties because Cuties are made for kids." Children aren't the ones running to the store to buy Cuties, but they do have an impact on what their parents are choosing to purchase, which are appealing to their children.

Doritos Locos: Taco Bell brilliantly combined two existing items into one with great results. The traditional menu item, the Taco Supreme, and blended it with Doritos chips, whoa la, a new item was born. Consumers love it. In just a short year, Taco Bell sold over $1m of these. That's lots of tacos!

Webit: This startup company based in Detroit provides couples five handheld video cameras for their wedding ceremony and celebration. Family and friends are encouraged to shoot footage. The cameras go back and Webit edits the footage. This is a huge savings for the already expensive cost of getting married. There is no need for the traditional videographer. This is brilliant, but the CEO of this entrepreneurial company had no budget for marketing. She thought about how she could help her clients, mostly brides who are fascinated with Pinterest. The CEO started pinning home décor, recipes, vacation, and of course, all things wedding. Big hotels and wedding planners caught on and pinned images about Wedit with a description of the company's services. The effect was HUGE. Last year Webit has a 388% increase in sales. And the number continues to grow.

Lululemon: I'm a fan. People know this brand of high-end workout clothes, centered on yoga and other lifestyle exercise alternatives. Did you know the Lululemon stores double for a yoga studio? This creates community involvement, constant engagement with their customer, and exemplifies its brand from within. They are offering a service, before sales.

My son is a marathon runner. The store where he buys his sneakers, Scranton Running Company, offers a program where the runner will receive a perfect fitting shoe for his style and abilities. They are more than a sneaker store. They provide workout classes; organize community programs where all the proceeds go to supporting local athletics. It's their way of constant engagement with their customer and demonstrating their brand from within. Customers are kept current on local, state, and national events through social networking. Yes they keep some of the old method for marketing, and they agree that their business took off once they implemented a constant program for C.S.I. Change, Sustain, and continually innovating.

The key to creative marketing is serving your customer, before sales. Know your audience and fishing where the fish swim. Clients will always ask, who do I call, where do I find my audience. Simple, know where they hang out and get there! You can always tell someone about your product. Boring! Turn your marketing system up side down and get to the core of your passion. Then rally your team around your creative solution to creatively market to the world! You have a product, the world needs your product—What are you waiting for?

What is the definition of entrepreneur?

The definition of entrepreneur is a "person who organizes and operates a business or businesses, taking on greater than normal financial risks in order to do so." If there were no profit, then how could you turn the lights on in the morning, hire high-quality employees, conduct employee training, or continue to develop your product or service? The cost of running a business can be enormous. Today, consumers are keener than ever before, and when making a purchasing decision or deciding where to be philanthropic, they will do their research. Good or bad, they will find information about you on the World Wide Web. Heck, before a customer completes a transaction with your organization, feedback will be found immediately on their social networks. Their circle of friends will know about your services NOW!

We don't believe in get rich programs - only in hard work, adding value and serving others. We just want to help by giving great content, direction, and strategies that move you forward. Our programs are intended to help you share your message with a wider audience and to make a difference in the world while growing your business. Before

we delve into the core information, please note that I don't know of any magic wand or secret sauce, it's up to you to make the magic happen. To be successful requires a consistent, persistent, determined, and intentional system. You need to find your balance. Now it's time to discover how to *Marketing Masters.*

creative
marketing strategies

C reative marketing focuses on service, not sales. Traditionally, a sale was sales, "we've got great stuff, buy from us." What makes you stand out from your competition? Steve Jobs said, "you need to stop focusing on doing it better than your competition — **you need to do it different.**" Today marketing isn't just advertising. Marketing isn't something that happens when you have a finished product. You need to market before your product goes to market. As an entrepreneur you will find many of your products will come from feedback you receive from your customers. Creative marketing is how you strategically convince the world to buy your products or services.

Let me be clearer—the definition of creative marketing is someone who can convince the world to buy your products with the least amount of money, in the least amount of time possible. This takes creativity.

Hilton Hotels strategically listen on Twitter. When someone types in "I'm looking for help" Hilton employees respond. The help may not have anything to do with Hilton, this is a creative marketing strategy they are doing successfully. Because when looking for a hotel who will they think of first? Hilton, the hotel that helped!

My creative marketing strategies have stood out time and tie again when I was working at the Chamber of Commerce. One of the number one benefits why an entrepreneur chooses to join a Chamber is for the healthcare program. One week after joining the Chamber the program came to a screeching halt. Chamber members were dropping like flies. The membership dropped by 20%. I quickly rallied the team, included Chamber members and volunteers, asking one question — beside healthcare what benefit can we provide members? Before long it came to me — **marketing, networking, business building, etc. with little or no marketing budget necessary.** The plan I implemented increased membership beyond the 20% loss. Members had seen a benefit using our creative marketing system beyond healthcare coverage.

When you sell you have a customer today. When you are serving (helping) your customer -you have a customer for life. That's the system Hilton is using. They are helping people and creating loyal customers for life. When you're helpful you keep your customers close. They will follow you on your social media sites: Facebook, Twitter, Linkedin, Pinterest, and Bookmark your website.

If you want to stay relevant, you need to always be transforming yourself. We talk about the technology revolution where a business had to transform to using the telephone, fax, World Wide Web, and now social media. You need to be relevant and available 24x7. We are no more the masters to servant business structure. You must develop a peer-to-peer marketing system. Customers have skin in the game. **They are talking about you. What are they saying? Are you searching yourself and learning what your customers are saying about you?** They're not bashful. Your customer's have become reporters. They are talking about you faster, smarter, and more social. **It's the power of NOW**! Your business culture needs to be in alignment to succeed with the power of social media.

Creating your culture means-hiring people with a passion for your enterprise and continually learning. It's easy to teach someone a skill and leading them with passion.

Whether you embrace it or not, I hope you are, **social media is driving consumer purchases**. It doesn't matter if you're Hilton, UPS, or a small entrepreneurial business. **Consumers are driving purchases through social media.** Focus on the digital trends. When you're on Facebook your posting a message to your circle. Your loyal customers are then sharing to their circle, so on, and so on. The circle grows and grows. **Social media is where personal and professional relationships collide.** People are learning about you across the globe. If you have good content, good service, you will get sales.

Here is the key; you need to promote your usefulness for them first. Traditionally we would promote our services first and foremost. There was no usefulness for them. Because consumers are smarter you need to focus on how you are helping them.

I talked about the creative marketing system we implemented for Chamber members. The basis of the program was helping the community businesses by introducing them to other businesses, potential customers. We did this relatively cheap. We purchased large scissors, like the ones used for ribbon cuttings. Each Wednesday we would meet with selected members that would be renewing within the upcoming three months, members who joined in the last three months, and non-members. The members, ambassadors, were calling the Chamber asking to be part of this program. It was no cost to them, except for their time. **Imagine the ability to creatively market your enterprise to hundreds of potential customers visiting your business and getting free press**. The only rule, as a visitor you were not allowed to promote your business. The spotlight was on the host. You can always go back and introduce yourself. This program was a SUCCESS!

Now take **those loyal customer's and introduce them to your social media platform and your circle will explode** — only when you promote your usefulness for them. We did have one more rule; you must be honest and authentic in your approach. Through social media you are showing-up and letting your customers into your personality.

I've worked with clients in both the private and public sector who are afraid of social media. They don't want people to know what they're doing. Yes, I agree we don't need to tell the world what we are having for lunch. There is however, a place for social media in your business. **If you're not in, how will your customers find you**? Use this platform to your advantage. Social Media could be dangerous only if you allow it to be. You don't have to be a social media expert. This platform will be your friend and you will become a content expert in your field. This technology and the data you are able to collect will help you in volumes increase your business.

Warning, depending on your business you may still need to implement the ole' school of creative marketing. Beware; your customers may still require a personal touch, such as a telephone call. If you only go the route of ole' school marketing you run the risk of failure. Which ever path you take, remember to **focus on service, not sales**. Have patience while you develop your creative marketing system. Your marketing strategies will help you achieve success. And success is the best motivator of all.

innovate
captivate convert

You're going to hear the same from many entrepreneurs. We have a small budget, we don't have the luxury of time, and we certainly don't have the resources for what sounds like an impossible task of creating a creative marketing system. Unfortunately, many will quit before getting started while waiting for that someone to invest in their company. How many of you considered going on Shark Tank? Good luck with that.

Don't give up hope. You have many tools at your disposal and many companies have used these tools successfully. You just need to know where to look. Before you get started you need to think about your marketing strategies from the time of product inception. Think of it this way. You're ready to build your dream home. Before the first hammer meet the nail you need to decide on your home design. You don't need to worry about the kitchen cabinet handles just yet, but how where will the cabinets be placed? Likewise, don't waste time and money - think about your marketing strategy when you are designing your product and services.

Let me share several case studies I located from Marketing Profs (2014). Each business from different markets and different size revenue, found a unique way to **innovate** their products or service, which **captivated** their market. Each business began to see a great impact on how they were able to **convert** a brand-new audience, while sustaining current customers.

Recent Case Studies (Marketing Profs, 2014)

Case Study #1
> **Company:** Roberts & Durkee, P.A.
> **Contact:** C. David Durkee, Partner
> **Location:** Coral Gables, Fla.
> **Industry:** Law **Annual revenue:** Confidential
> **Number of employees:** Confidential

Quick Read

In June, The Wall Street Journal reported a surge in social-media use by law firms interested in connecting with potential class-action plaintiffs. But if you take a closer look, you'll see that many of the approaches used represent viable marketing lessons for businesses of all types.

Take, for example, the case of Roberts & Durkee, P.A., a Florida-based firm. It has effectively created widespread public awareness around the problem of toxic Chinese drywall and has assisted affected homeowners on multiple levels while generating valuable exposure for the firm and facilitating relations with potential clients.

Not all businesses can easily link their marketing efforts to this particular problem, but the firm's strategy, along with the individual tactics pursued, offer some best-practices for launching a well-trafficked corporate blog and establishing yourself as a trusted authority in the marketplace.

Read more: http://www.marketingprofs.com/casestudy/2010/9259/how-one-companys-thought-leadership-content-is-driving-new-business-exposure#ixzz37Tm6LZVP

Case Study #2

Company: Coconut Bliss
Contact: Larry Kaplowitz, co-founder
Location: Eugene, Ore.
Industry: Food, B2C
Annual revenue: $5,000,000
Number of employees: 11

Quick Read

Has the world of marketing come full circle? As social media turns what we consider to be "traditional" on its end by empowering the people and endorsing two-way conversations over broadcast messaging, more brands are realizing the importance of methods employed long before the days of mass media, mass messaging, and mass efficiencies—that is, straightforward, one-to-one relationship-building.

In fact, a recent study from IBM, which interviewed more than 1,500 CEOs, general managers, and senior public-sector leaders from 60 countries and 33 industries, found that the majority of company leaders (88%) view deeper customer relationships as the most important dimension of realizing their business strategies in the next five years.

Perhaps it's time for big business to take a page from the little guys— such as Eugene, Ore.-based Coconut Bliss. Its grassroots, customer-focused efforts have enabled the company to establish a nationwide presence in just a few short years, while nurturing an incredibly strong and genuine passion among customers that could never have been achieved through ad impressions.

Read more: http://www.marketingprofs.com/casestudy/2010/9402/ how-a-mom-and-pop-operation-turned-itself-into-a-cult-brand#ixzz37TmFCJfY

Case Study #3
> **Company:** C. F. Martin & Co.
> **Contact:** Dick Boak, Artist & Public Relations
> **Location:** Nazareth, Pa.
> **Industry:** Musical instruments
> **Annual revenue:** $93,000,000
> **Number of employees:** 825

Quick Read

Economic downturns come and go—every 11 years or so, according to Dick Boak's calculations. He's a historian at heart, and during his long tenure at C. F. Martin & Co., maker of fine guitars, he's seen a few dips—perhaps none as titanic as 2009's. But as keeper of the archives, he understands that the current downturn isn't the first, nor the last, the company must endure.

And endure the company has, for 177 years—through the Great Depression, World Wars, and a Civil War—outlasting countless fads and trends to become the oldest-surviving acoustic-instrument maker in the world.

The keys to its success? High-quality products, adaptability, and a willingness to learn from the past—all of which came into play during the plight of 2009.

Read more: http://www.marketingprofs.com/casestudy/2010/9399/lessons-from-martin-guitars-three-ways-to-survive-a-downturn#ixzz37TmP3ytc

Case Study #4
Company: Dr. Helaine Smith, DMD
Contact: Dr. Helaine Smith, DMD
Location: Boston
Industry: Dentistry, B2C
Annual revenue: Confidential
Number of employees: Confidential

Quick Read

Like many service professionals, Dr. Helaine Smith, DMD, is more than a dentist. She's also a small-business owner who must attend to more than continuing-education credits—including her own marketing and promotion—if she is to keep her business going and growing.

And like most small businesses, particularly those in the medical field, credibility is key. So, not long ago, Smith made it her personal mission to establish herself as a dental authority in the public eye.

Some might think that jumping on the "sex sells" bandwagon may not be the best way to go about that. Smith is living proof, however, that if approached the right way in conjunction with other awareness-generating tactics such as effective search-engine optimization (SEO), sex can be the tantalizing introduction that gets people to listen up and take notice.

Read more: http://www.marketingprofs.com/casestudy/2010/9398/seo-and-sex-a-recipe-for-success#ixzz37TmWL500

get to know your customer

People buy from people they know, like, and trust. And people give to people, not to products, unless you have a must have product. Your ability to market and to create a positive image of your business in the marketplace is essential. Remember, your success largely depends upon your ability to connect with people, and show how you are serving, not selling.

So, what stops most people from being successful at increasing sales? A deep-rooted fear of rejection; in other words, the thing that's getting in your way of success is YOU.

How does somebody know what they want
when they've never seen it.
—Steve Jobs

Fear of rejection is human nature. But did you know that you have a choice in how you handle rejection? It's true. You can choose to allow rejection to pull you down or you can choose to allow rejection to pick you up. It's all about the attitude you choose to embrace.

How do I achieve and maintain a positive attitude, despite any rejection I may face?

Attitude is a state of mind. Whether your attitude is positive or negative is a choice. No matter what's happening around you, no matter what kind of rejection you're facing, you're in control of your attitude, and you determine what your attitude is.

We all have a negative sense and a positive sense that can shape our attitude. A negative sense is based in fear. It's about procrastination, self-doubt, uncertainty, and doom. It's what makes people say things like, "I'm so unlucky" or "I never catch a break" or "The sky is falling." Do you know anyone like this?

Have you ever gone to a church picnic or school event where there was a raffle? How many times do you hear people say, "I never win anything"? When I go to those events, I always win something. I don't really try; it just happens that way. I think it's because I choose to see the possibilities rather than the obstacles.

If your mental attitude continually says, "I'm unlucky," it's time to turn that around. Focus on your purpose, presence, psychology, productivity, and persuasion and develop a kick ass creative marketing system.

A positive sense is based in opportunity. It's about self-confidence, determination, achievement, winning, success, good fortune, and a sense of a sunny day. I've found that you can transform a rainy, miserable day into a sunny day at any time. You just have to choose to do so.

Here's a quick story to illustrate the power of a positive attitude. When I lost my position as CEO of the Girl Scouts. At about the same time I learned that I was adopted… Dad was not who he said he was. When I received the news I was in shock, disbelief, and, without realizing it, this added to my depression. Not the clinical version, but I became sick, had nine surgeries in two-years. I soon realized it was my attitude that was causing me to be ill. I turned myself around by shifting my attitude. One step I took was to go back to school. My life goal was to complete my bachelor's degree. As of this writing, it's been six years. Today, I have completed my Bachelor' in Business Administration. I also earned my Master in Business Science, and Master in Public Administration, Speech and Marketing. Yeah me!

If you ask how I overcame this life calamity, I will tell you it was because of a change in my attitude. Turning lemons to lemonade! I decided I was going to fight the illness and not let it or anyone bring me down. I refused to feel sorry for myself or behave like a sick person. The entire time I was battling my illness I continued going to school and learning as much as I could about people, organizational behavior, and politics—even when I was recovering from my surgeries. Keeping a positive attitude the entire time made all the difference.

How do I focus my creative marketing system on a specific market?

It's difficult for me to answer without knowing your business. However, 99.9 percent of the times you need to focus on a specific market. If you have a product for an "esoteric" market and your prospects are not easily identified, then you have to market your products far-and-wide - yeah for technology! Traditionally, once you found your customer, you would have to charge lots of dollars to recover your traditional marketing cost. With technology and the use of your social networks, creative marketing is made simple. The only additional cost would be shipping—and that you pass onto your customer.

If you're a doctor or dentist - creative marketing to the rescue. The use of social media still applies, however dentist can be 100% identified in each country. However, a creative dentist will specialize in a specific area. Locally, we have a children's dentist. Can he work on adults, he sure can. He chooses to specialize in children's dentistry. He is known as the entertaining dentist. I've never been there, but I heard he pretty much makes it a celebration for a child when they visit him for dental work. His uses my creative marketing system by promoting his practice through his social networks, which includes fun, filled days at his office.

Is your creative marketing system labor-intense?
What is easier? Offering a website with all the marathon runners scores or allowing users from all around the world to follow their favorite athlete in real-time action? And by providing this application you get more traffic to your website?

That's exactly what many marathon organizers are using during races. I was able to follow my son and his girlfriend while they ran the Boston Marathon. Not only did I follow, I would receive periodic updates on their advancement.

I am a member of the National Speakers Association. At this year's conference the association provided an app where we would upload our selected programs. The best part, each morning I would be reminded of the day's program and meeting location. Awesome sauce!

Creative marketing avoids labor-intensive marketing. You may have to reorganize you daily schedule from creating labor-intensive billboard, or radio or print advertisements to creatively marketing your business on your social media sites. And its not just marketing your business, its what you can do to turn consumers into customers. Become like Hilton and search Twitter providing help to others. Even if its not about your business.

If nothing else, social networks make it a whole lot easier to get in front of your customer's. When you provide a service customers will find you.

Ole' Creative Marketing Strategies to stay in touch with your customers

- Snail Mail (newsletters, brochures, letters)
- Telephone calls (telemarketers)
- Email
- Purchase a list of relevant prospects
- Sales force | Pay high commissions
- Billboards
- Send out press releases
- Exhibit at trade shows

New Creative Marketing Strategies to stay in touch with your customers

- Blogging and writing articles
- Twitter | Tweet Chats
- Facebook
- LinkedIn
- Pinterest
- YouTube
- Strategic Article Placement
- Google Plus | Google Hangouts
- Comment | Comment | Comment on other people's Blogs

Don't ignore the ole' fashion way of marketing and embrace the new marketing strategies. You have no geographical limitations. I have a telephone exchange for Pennsylvania, a landline phone with a California exchange, and offices in multiple locations. No one knows where I really am at any moment in time. What my clients do know— I'm there for them.

Because we are a virtual society and we need to be quick, you could set up a network of sales people (affiliates). These are people who represent your business in the marketplace. You could accept credit card and cash payments in minutes. Your goal isn't to be great at social networking; your goal is to be great at building your business because of social networking. Social media is another tool for your business toolbox.

Many entrepreneurs pay thousands of dollars creating their website and business logos. Trust me when I say I paid peanuts to have my website and logo designed. You don't need to go broke to create your brand. Start somewhere. You could always go back and make changes later. Most importantly determine how you will serve your customers, and not sell.

When creating your website make your page a resource to your customers. Using desired keywords when posting articles. Become the leading authority in your specific area. Search Engine Optimization (SEO) was a foreign term to many of us 2 days ago when we were using the ole' creative marketing strategies. SEO is extremely important to make words stand out. The first 256 words on your website carry the most weight. Bold your main keywords and when applicable, make those keywords into links. I can't do it here—how would you link from my book? I'm sure its coming in the next evolution of technology.

Capture your potential customer's information and stay in touch with them. You offer help to someone looking for a restaurant in New York City. Now you have their contact information. BINGO! They are now added to your network. The next time you give a restaurant review or talk about your services they will remember that you helped them out in a jam.

I know many people will send out cards or postcards via technology. Personally, I prefer to send out cards handwritten by me. I don't ask my assistant—I write them out. I believe this adds an extra personal touch. I receive thank you cards from a service and I know immediately it is printed by machine. Sorry, I quickly discard these cards. Writing a personal card is my way of standing out and letting my customer know they are appreciated. I want to be known as the easiest person to work with. When I'm working with an event planner I tell them...and I live by my promise!

- I don't dance
- I don't sing
- I am a disruptive social media content expert working with entrepreneurs who are ready to Change create Sustainability and !nnovate (C.S.!)
- I am organized, on time, considerate and easy to work with.
- My goal is to be the best speaker an event planner works with, EVER!

What other ways can I capture an audience and increase revenue?
Create an affiliate program. An affiliate program will allow you to attract more customers. Affiliates know how to find customers for your digital products. Affiliate programs are one of the best secrets in business. An entrepreneur can easily reap the benefits of creating a team who sells for you. The secret is to multiply your product sales by a factor of ten or more.

Affiliate programs quickly convert more customers in your direction. You need to implement a quick ordering system, and be selective of the information you are asking your customers.

You can also become an affiliate of other entrepreneurs and public business. I'm an affiliate of Amazon. Each time a customer enter

Amazon through my website portal—I get a commission. The range of commissions is 1% up to 75% of the sale. An associate of mine shares his monthly affiliate commission. His monthly average is $38,000 and that number continues to grow. ClickBank.com is a great resource for setting up your affiliate program.

Is implementing a creative marketing system measurable?
I'm going to start by asking a series of questions I learned from a coaching associate.

Q's #1: The desired results and outcomes you are focused on.
1. What are the most important results you are focusing on this year?
2. What are the biggest opportunities you want to take advantage of?
3. What are the biggest challenges you are facing?

Q's #2: The specific and important metrics worth using for designing success.
1. What measurements will tell you this has been highly successful and meaningful to your business?
2. What are the most important measurements you will use to gauge progress and success?
3. How well are your current measurements of success working?

Q's #3: Establish the value worth investing in—time and money. When price is not an issue the value is clear. Quantify what achieving your significant; high-impact priority outcomes would be worth to your business.
1. What would achieving these metrics be worth (consider both objective and subjective)? Subjective evaluations regularly produce an objective trend.

2. What kind of increases over what you would normally expect would these results produce?

3. What would it cost you if you failed to achieve these results?

When determining your ROI count all variables. Change one variable at a time so you can easily see if the change was for the better. Avoid surprises and keep track of all aspects of your business.

Can you handle a rush of a 5,000 queries and then have nothing the next day? When you are developing your creative marketing system, tailor the program to your business abilities to optimize all available resources.

know what you want

O ne of the keys to becoming a successful entrepreneur is to know what you want—what you really, really want. That means you need to set S.M.A.R.T. goals.

A goal is nothing more than a dream with a plan and a deadline. Creating that plan and deadline around your dream is all about S.M.A.R.T. goal setting.

S.M.A.R.T. stands for

- **Specific**—A specific goal has a much greater chance of being accomplished than a general goal. Goals must be clear and unambiguous; vagaries and platitudes have no place in goal setting.

- **Measurable**—Establish concrete criteria for measuring progress toward the attainment of each goal you set. When you measure your progress, you stay on track, reach your target dates, and experience the exhilaration of achievement that spurs you on to the continued effort required to reach your goal.

- **Attainable**—Goals must be realistic and attainable. The best goals require you to stretch a bit to achieve them, but they aren't extreme.

- **Relevant**—To be relevant, a goal must represent an objective toward which you are both willing and able to work. Your goal is probably relevant if you truly believe that it can be accomplished.

- **Time-Oriented**—If you want to accomplish a goal, how soon do you want to accomplish it? "Some day" won't work. But if you anchor it within a time frame, "by January 1st," then you've set your unconscious mind into motion to begin working on the goal.

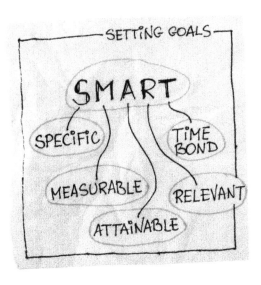

With the idea of S.M.A.R.T. goals in mind, ask yourself

- What are the most important results I am focusing on this year?
- What are the biggest opportunities I want to take advantage of?
- What measurements will tell me my efforts are highly successful?
- What would it cost me if I failed to achieve my desired results?

Write your answers down! If you don't write them down you're going to forget your answers quickly. In fact, the main reason people don't achieve their goals is because they don't write them down!

After you have your goals written down, do your own personal SWOT analysis. What are your strengths, weaknesses, opportunities, and threats that are going to either help you or get in your way of reaching your goals? Write these down, too.

Should I share my goals with others?

Depending on your business structure and your goals, you may want to share your goals with others. Perhaps someone can help you achieve the goal in some way (by providing resources, leads, etc.). Or maybe having some outside accountability, like a coach or join a mastermind group, will keep you motivated and accountable towards achieving your goals. Of course, if you don't feel comfortable sharing your goals, for whatever reason, then don't. Don't put any undue stress on yourself.

My goal seems so big. What's the best way to approach it?

No matter how large or small your goal is, create an action plan for attaining it. Break the goal down into manageable chunks and then state deadlines for completing each segment of the larger goal.

For example, if you make a goal to lose weight, you know you need to exercise and go on a diet. So your first segment of the goal is to create a weekly diet plan. Then, in addition to that weekly plan, the next segment of your goal is to join a gym. Once you have the membership, the next segment of your goal is to actually go to the gym, and so on. So it's about setting smaller goals that enable you to achieve your ultimate goal.

No matter what your goal is, keep it clearly in sight—both literally and figuratively. Post your goals on your office wall so you can look at them every day. Remember, you get what you focus on. What are you going to focus on today?

What are the rewards and consequences?

Making a commitment to your goal in writing is the first step to achievement. The next step is identifying the benefits you will experience once you achieve your goals. List your rewards for achieving your goals and the consequences that you will want to avoid if your goals are not met. Become emotional with your goals and avoid the roadblocks. Persistence is key to success.

get a coach

i 've had several mentors or coaches in my life. At the time, I didn't think of these people as coaches or mentors, but looking back now, I see that they really were.

No matter where you are in your business, don't be afraid to seek out a coach.[1] Look for somebody who appears to be a successful entrepreneur—a person you admire or would want to emulate. You could also seek out a professional coach—someone who charges a fee for their coaching services. Either way, it'll be an investment in yourself you'll never regret.

---

1   You can get more information about *Green Apples Impact Academy* and one-on-one coaching with Connie Pheiff by completing a contact form found at www.conniepheiffspeaks.com or send an email to TEAMPHEIFF@conniepheiffspeaks.com.

What are some guidelines to keep in mind when working with a coach?

- Use your coach wisely. Don't use or abuse your privileges with them. Your coach is going to take pride in your growth.

- Acknowledge your coach, and show that you did what they suggested. Did it work or not?

- Share freely with your coach. Don't hold back. If you want their guidance, they need to know how best to help you.

- Let them help you. You will have days when you're feeling down. Your coach's job is to help pull you back up. When they extend their hand, take it.

- Respect their wisdom. You're asking this person for help because they've "been there and done that." When they give you guidance, take it, no matter how contrary to your thinking it may seem. That's the point of having a coach—to have someone help you see things in different ways.

Throughout my career, coaches have been a major part of my success and growth. I wouldn't be where I am today without their support and guidance.

Does the coaching relationship always have to be a formal one?

The coaching may come from a formal coaching relationship, or it may come from someone who doesn't even realize they're being a coach to you.

For example, when I worked for the United States Chamber of Commerce, my boss was a wonderful coach, although he had no idea of it at the time, or so I thought. One of the best ways to learn is to sit and watch/listen to someone, and that's what I did with him. I would watch him make a fundraising call. Or I would watch him approach a Fortune 100 Entrepreneur in person, and I'd listen to what he'd say to them. Then I would mirror what he did, and I found it worked for me. So, although he didn't realize it, he was coaching me.

In fact, I learned one of my biggest lessons from watching that guy. Most successful entrepreneurs have heard that when you're asking for the money, the one who speaks first loses. I had never heard that before until I went to a meeting with my boss.

One day we were visiting a prospective donor, and after my boss had asked for the donation, he just sat there in silence. And he didn't make a sound. I was getting nervous. *Why isn't he saying anything?* I thought. *Why isn't he closing this?*

Finally, the prospective donor spoke. He said, "Okay. Here's my money."

Later, when I asked my boss why he sat there in silence, he said, "That's the art of asking. You make your ask, you make your case, you show the benefits, and then you stop talking." It was a lesson I never forgot.

Marketing Masters
- Ready
- Set
- GROW Your Market

You interact with so many people on a daily basis. Who are you taking advice from? Make sure you're learning from the right people.

What benefits would I receive by creating an Advisory Board?

One of the best creative marketing strategies is to develop an advisory board. Each board member should be a cheerleader in your corner who lets the marketplace know that your organization is the go-to business for whatever products or service you provide. The Tipping Point by

Malcolm Gladwell (2000), is a great read to learn more about that moment when your idea, trend, or social behavior crosses the threshold and spreads like wildfire. What's your tipping point?

There is no limit to your board's participation and creative marketing efforts. However, keep in mind that these are volunteers and they may have different interests or time constraints. Right from the get-go, make sure your board members are on board (pun intended!). Ask them to help with planning and executing your marketing plan.

Why Have an Advisory Board?

Entrepreneurs considering setting up an advisory board must answer two key questions:

1. Why are we establishing an advisory board?
2. What do we want from the board members?

Entrepreneurs may be seeking assistance with marketing to managing human resources to influencing the direction of regulators. Think carefully about your advisory board's purpose to ensure it will be structured to maximize its contribution to your business success.

Advisory Board is Priceless!

The decision to involve outsiders in your business can be a difficult step. Some entrepreneurs simply do not want to give up their control by establishing an advisory board with formal authority and responsibilities. Before coming to any conclusions keep in mind an advisory board enables you, the entrepreneur and business owner, to feel comfortable with the business of providing information to, and accepting advice from, an external group. You can get overwhelmed when you're in business by yourself. An advisory board gives you the comfort of being in business for yourself but not by yourself.

Multinational companies could benefit from having local companies carry on their business in a particular foreign jurisdiction (in organizational, tax or other ways). That same multi-national could be hesitant to surrender meaningful authority to an outside group of directors of the local company. In such a case, an advisory board can address the realities of operating in a different location, with different cultural and business norms and perhaps in a different language, without any loss of control.

Formalizing advice

Entrepreneurs driving enterprises often find themselves lonely. For some, the issue may be that they have yet to build trust in any person or group to provide ongoing, meaningful guidance. For others, the complexity and speed of their business makes it difficult to reach out for help on any particular topic. We are human. Would you rather spend hours explaining to someone else the "how to's" of your business, or jump in and do it yourself. Entrepreneurs are do-it yourselfers. We need to learn to let go.

In these and similar cases, advisory boards provide the degree of consistency, longevity and background knowledge that can allow advisory board members to know enough and have enough interest that they can advise reliably on particular issues. Having an advisory board position and receiving compensation for the position (or being committed in some other way) help to ensure that a request for assistance will be taken seriously and that thoughtful advice will be provided.

Safe Harbours

Advisory board members are often volunteers and need to be treated the same as staff members. When a volunteer is working on your time, policies and procedures must be followed. I had to fire volunteers on several occasions. One of the firings caused such a mess with the organization that we had to get an attorney involved. The volunteer just refused to leave. Your volunteers are the face of the organization. If you have a volunteer who is badmouthing the organization or you, get to the bottom of the issue right away. If you don't deal with the issue head-on, it will only fester and get worse.

Of course, have fun with your volunteers, but remember you, your employees, and your volunteers are the face of the organization. I would suggest no pole dancing on weekends.

CHAPTER 8

go viral
marketing

a good creative marketer provides a service before telling everyone about their business and its mission. That means you have to approach the marketplace—both new and established—and consistently provide a service. Keep your focus on the digital trends. Social Media is where consumers become customers. Even if someone has bought your product or services every year for the past decade, you need to keep the conversation going so that your business continues to build momentum and remain at the forefront. How are you going to be different than your competition?

Most people you'll be contacting have either shown an interest in the organization in the past, or they have took notice in some way—either through a direct sale, online purchase, or have become familiar with your products/services. This happens in your social network. Therefore, you're technically dealing with warm contacts rather than cold ones. That alone should ease any fears, increase your confidence, and make your sales easier.

Provide a service, not sales.
—**Connie Pheiff**

What's the best way to get information to the marketplace?

Many entrepreneurs think they need a glitzy brochure and other sales materials to present to potential customers. Today's consumer is smarter and can find information on your products immediately — at rapid speed. What you need is to be intentional with your marketing strategies, which include social media. Billboards, television, print advertising still

 have its place in marketing. But if you want to capture a higher percentage of the marketplace then you need to invest more time in social media outlets. My best advice is to start by learning the needs of your market demographics.

Social media is a low-cost marketing option, but remember that the older generation hasn't embraced it as readily. So if you rely primarily on social media to get your information out there, you're missing out on a large pool of potential customers.

When it comes to disseminating your information, the best approach is to have multiple balls in the air. In other words, if you know someone wants to see a brochure, then send them one. If you know someone loves social media, then connect with them there. If you know someone prefers phone calls, then pick up the phone and call them. I find the best approach is through my social networks and the old fashioned way— a face-to-face personal touch. But when trying to reach the marketing office to discuss a corporate sponsorship, your marketing strategy will be a bit different.

What's the Entrepreneur guru's secret weapon for getting the word out?

Research your demographics and know everything you need to know about your target market. Be specific about your product and services. Don't try to be everything to everyone. I did and it doesn't work.

Position yourself as a thought leader. Exploit the Internet and social media. In the 1990's, the Internet may have been one of the best things that happened for entrepreneurs. In the last few years, social media may be the "new" best thing. The combination of the two are what is bringing people to my website, which causes the phone to ring with clients and media, which creates speaking engagements and public relations. Here are my current top ten ways to use the Internet and social media.

1. Blogging and writing articles
2. Twitter | Tweet Chats
3. Facebook
4. LinkedIn
5. Pinterest
6. YouTube
7. Strategic Article Placement
8. Google Plus | Google Hangouts
9. Comment | Comment | Comment on other people's Blogs
10. The traditional emailed newsletter

I bet your asking when do I have time for all of this. Let me remind you this has been my best no-cost, or sometimes very-low-cost way to get exposure.

First thing in the morning, while I'm still drinking my morning coffee I look at LinkedIn, Facebook, Twitter and Google alerts. I am intentional with my time limitations. If your not careful you can get lost in cyberspace.

Here is another suggestion. Hire a virtual assistant. Provide your assistant an outline of your weekly blogs or just a theme and let them run with it. The posts are written and scheduled release throughout the week. Virtual assistants can blog and write articles on your behalf. It's awesome! I see myself posting everyday—I'm fabulous!

I also find that picking up the phone and calling someone gets the results I want and expect. As an entrepreneur, you simply cannot have call reluctance. And if you're calling warm contacts, why should you fear calling them?

Can you keep a secret? Being an entrepreneur is hard work. There is no way around it. While I'm still spending time on the phone talking with clients, the amount of time I used to spend researching whom to call and then making the initial outbound calls is replaced with my social media strategies.

If you're calling a big customer, you'll want to schedule a time to meet with them face-to-face unless they are located on the other side of the pond. So you let them know right up-front: "I want to meet with you. All I need is 10 minutes of your time." Then you meet with them. That's how you get the information to them. It's about having the confidence to pick up the phone, to be direct, and to meet them face-to-face. If you can't do that, then someone else, your competition, will and ultimately get your customers business.

What's the best strategy to go Viral?
- Write articles about other people — **only when you have something nice to say!**

- Photo share
- Create a community and not just have visitors
- Ask your friends | colleagues to share your thoughts
- Let others "declare" you the leader in your industry
- Create a buzz
- By invitation only communities
- Create a sense of scarcity
- Make it newsworthy
- Develop symbiotic relationships

How do I get past appearing to have a hidden agenda?
Sometimes things are not what they appear to be - banks market themselves to be your 'friend.' "We'll help you get the financial support you deserve." When in fact, they want you to be late because that is how they are making money—on your late-fees.

Ray Kroc started one of the first successful burger chains that could be found around the globe. In fact McDonalds was intended to be a real-estate company.

Did you know that fashion shows are intended to sell perfume and t-shirts, not fancy clothes?

Apple Computers sells status and the opportunity to be different.

Starbucks builds self confidence by giving a man or woman the ability to stand firm for what he wants - Tall, dark, nonfat, cappuccino.

Dell managed to further optimize their e-commerce operation by reaching an agreement with the United States Postal Service where personal computers are delivered by truck to the Post Office and the client pick's up the shipment from there. This method of shipping creates a sense of safety for the customer because they are not home during delivery hours, cost savings for the customer, and better customer service for Dell products.

Kellogg's is a cereal brand, so why are they buying farms? Buying farms allows the business to have greater control of the product quality and have cheaper wheat prices they pass onto consumers.

Pixar was near failure when they decided instead of selling advanced workstations; they would use workstations internally to produce their movies. Their decision was a cost savings they were able to pass onto movie enthusiasts.

How do I play fair?

No one said you have to play fair. You need to be different. Stand out from the crowd. One way I stand out is through my radio show (Podcast) *Marketing Masters*. I was fortunate to be offered a seat in the captain's chair on Matrix Media. A Chicago-based radio syndication firm with credits includes Animal Planet Radio, Travel Channel Radio, The HGTV Design Minutes, and the NBA Radio Network.

Because of today's technology my radio show has a great reach. I am often interviewed on radio and the greatest reach was an interview by a show host based in England. His show was live 11 am England time. Because I am based in Los Angeles the time difference left me to be wide-awake at 2 am.

The benefit of hosting my own show is I can charge my competition to advertise, which in turn I use to cover my airtime expenses. I hold the prime advertising spot for promoting my programs.

How do I get noticed?

My best advice is consistency, be genuine, and be intentional. In addition to radio (podcast) get noticed by writing articles for newspaper columns and magazines. They are selling advertising, but always looking for content. When you're in the press it could carry certain credibility. I write for several columns throughout the year. My columns has been picked up, printed, and shared by numerous media outlets without my knowledge. I find out after the fact when a customer brings it to my attention. It's always great to hear your name in the news for something good—of course!

You can always ask your customers to promote your writings ad encourage them to provide feedback on your material. Testimonials are a great way to share your customer's thoughts with others. It adds credibility. This is all part of my creative marketing system.

get customers
to call you

et's say you've decided to secure a corporate sponsor; a business partner. New and experienced entrepreneurs always ask me, "How do I get to the right person? How do I get them to return my call?" The answer: be persistent.

It's rare that a potential sponsor will call you back immediately after your first attempt. Remember, they're busy (as are you). They have a company to run, a family to take care of, social obligations to fulfill, and a life to live. Unfortunately, you and your business are seldom at the top of their list of priorities. But the more persistent you are in your follow up, the greater your chances of getting a call back. A business partner is looking for instant gratification. They want to know who you are before speaking with you.

How can I provide instant gratification?

Use your creative marketing system to include a way to provide instant gratification. People want immediate results. When they go to your website they want to know what are you offering them. If you're asking them to sign up for your newsletter, offer something in return—instant gratification. For example, if you have a book, offer a download of your first chapter. Be creative, I'm sure you could come up with an idea to provide your customers instant gratification. If you don't, they may quickly lose interest in your products and services. When you give something away for free you become a destructive marketer to your competition.

What's the best way to build rapport with someone when I haven't even spoken to the person yet?

It's true that sponsors are more apt to call you back if they like you or feel a sense of connection with you or see a connection with your business. So how do you develop that before even speaking to them? One way is to leave a message about something important to them.

For example, I once was trying to reach a top Fortune 100 CEO who I knew was an avid fly fisherman. I had left several messages with no reply. About a month later, I learned that a fly-fishing convention was coming to town. So I called him again and left a message stating, "Hi, Jack. I called to let you know that there's a fly-fishing convention coming to town. I have the details about it. Call me back, and I'll fill you in."

A few hours later, he called me back. Of course, I gave him the details of the convention, and then I made my "ask" for my business. He wrote me a check that day.

Another way is to find someone who knows the person you're trying to reach. Then when you leave a message, you can say, "Hi, Monica. Lisa Peterson from the University said I should call you. She mentioned that your organization is trying to [state something you've learned they are trying to do that ties to what your organization does]. My organization has similar interests. I'd love to discuss this more with you."

Find whatever triggers you can that will create desire and interest in the other person. They are asking themselves "What's in it for me" (WIIFM). That's what prompts a return call.

What's a good approach for timing follow-up phone calls?

No one wants to appear like a stalker, calling a sponsor every day. My advice is to call three times within a two-week period. If there's no reply, then let it go for a week or two. Psychologically, this makes people wonder, "Why isn't she calling me anymore?"

Be patient and use the time to connect on Twitter, Facebook, and LinkedIn. Write articles about their business (positive of course), and then when you call again they will remember you are the one who wrote a compelling story about them.

After that break of a week or two, call again, and this time relates the message to something the person has an interest in, such as, "Hi. I haven't heard from you. Did you know that X is happening in the community? You need to be a part of that. Give me a call, and I can fill you in."

If you still don't receive a response, don't give up. Continue sharing articles on your media networks. There just may be a story that resonates with them. You don't want to be seen as a stalker, but a great business leader willing to serve others.

Is it always a phone call? Can't I just send an email?

You can certainly send an email. The problem is that most busy executives get literally hundreds of emails each day, so there's a high chance yours will get lost. Of course, if you've tried calling for months and can't get a reply, then by all means send an email. Good luck with getting a response.

Think about your inbox. How many emails do you get in a week, in a day, or in the last hour? My inbox is continually working overtime. I will skim through my inbox three times a day, unless I'm waiting for an important message. Even when I try to shut down my outlook, I continue to receive messages. I read a small percentage of the messages and the others go to the delete box.

If you're comfortable sending an email, try to attach an article of interest so the person sees value in opening your message. Add something creative to your subject line. Then you can call and say, "Hi. I thought you might like to know that [insert whatever the pertinent article topic is you're going to send]. I'm going to email you an article about it. Take a look and give me a call." In your message direct the reader to your website where you have the article—now they know who you are.

If you still don't get a reply, you can call and leave a message stating, "I sent you a great article about X. I hope you've had a chance to read it. I have some ideas about it, too. Give me a call."

Do whatever you can to pique their interest. What do you know about your customer that you can use to build interest and rapport?

Because executives are busy and receive numerous emails they will have their messages sent directly to their assistant—the dreaded gatekeeper. Assistants are no longer only responsible for receiving and screening telephone calls for their boss; they are also responsible for the supervision of email messages and social media networks sites.

How do I get past the gatekeeper when I call?

If you're calling someone at a corporation, lets say to speak with the marketing executive about your compelling sponsorship proposal; chances are the person you need to reach will have an assistant, a gatekeeper. As you know, this person's job is to carefully screen all calls and make sure that only the ones his or her boss really wants will get through. That's why you want to always be polite and professional to the gatekeeper. Get this person on your side by addressing him or her by name and being friendly.

You can read many sales books on "techniques" for getting past the gatekeeper, but I suggest a simpler approach. Rather than playing games or using sales techniques, just be up front with the gatekeeper.

Here is a one approach:

Gatekeeper:	Hello Mr. Jones Office, this is Sarah, may I help you?
You:	Good morning Sarah, Is this the marketing office?
Gatekeeper:	Yes, how may I help you?
You:	I'm calling Mr. Jones to discuss the procedures for submitting a sponsorship proposal.
Gatekeeper:	I'm sorry Mr. Jones is not available.
You:	Sarah, What is the best time to reach Mr. Jones?
Gatekeeper:	I take all his messages can I help you?
You:	Yes you can. I understand your company supports entrepreneurs and I'm call to find out how to submit a sponsorship proposal. Perhaps you will be the best person to help me. Do you have a minute; I would love to share my products and services? [Share a few tidbits about your business. The goal is to pique the interest of the gatekeeper).
Gatekeeper:	We have a process for submitting sponsorship proposals. You can find the guidelines on our website.
You:	Sarah, Can I send my proposal directly to your attention?

"Sarah, Can you suggest where I may get a copy of your sponsorship proposal guidelines?" You're not selling—you are asking. You're serving Sarah, not selling. Yes, it really is as easy as that. Be up front and genuine, and you'll get your information out there. The more you make the calls, the more comfortable you will become.

Ultimately, the more you know about your market, the more creative marketing strategies you embrace, the more your customers will call you. Find out as much as you can about your customer, about their needs, and about their passion. Who are you going to ask today?

funding source

I have a small budget, what suggestions can you provide to help with my financial resources?

t here are always cheaper ways to growing your business. Sometimes it's good to have a limited budget. You want to be cautious of moral hazards. When you have a lot of money or time you end up wasting valuable resources. Force yourself to think in creative ways and to assume there is not a lot of money and time. Nobody can hide in a 6-day project, whereas, in a 6-month project people go on vacation, etc.

When you're tight on cash or not start looking for corporate sponsors. Think of a corporate sponsor as your business partner. Maybe you don't qualify for corporate sponsorships, or successfully engaged an investor on Shark Tank, but securing corporate sponsorships is easier than you think. Yes, this is a system that I highly recommend to all my clients. Think of it this way, NASCAR gets corporate sponsors, why can't you? Remember, to gain a corporate partner you need to use your creative marketing system the same way you would promote your products and services.

Let me keep it simple, if you don't have a serious offering, don't attempt to write a sponsorship. I come across too many wanna-be entrepreneurs who are simply in it as a hobby. Even the Federal Government says that if you are not making a business profit between 3-5 years, then it's a hobby. Potential funders follow the same criteria.

Creating a sponsorship without motivation is not a productive use of your time. If your passion is more of a hobby, then you may need to find another source for funding your project. Such as

1. RocketHub – powers donation-based funding for a wide variety of creative projects.
2. CrowdFunder – a platform for businesses with a growing social network of investors, tech startups, small businesses, and social enterprises. This platform offers a blend of donation-based and investment Crowdfunding from individuals and angel investors.
3. Indiegogo – maintains a tighter focus and curates creative projects approved for this site. Such as donation-based fundraising campaigns for most, such as music, hobbyists, personal finance needs, charities, and like me I used this platform to raise awareness and funding for my book *The Art of the Ask*…get into your fundraising groove.

4. Kickstarter – provides a site where projects raise donation-based funding. Projects range and offer a pre-selling of new products. This site is not for charities or personal financing needs.

These platforms are great for the hobbyists. However, this level of donations does not translate into success by any measure. Certainly many of these platforms are beneficial, but do the entrepreneurs truly understand the role of marketing in having a successful sponsorship campaign? I am confident that many are only hobbyists and with the wrong motivation.

Case #1

It's time to get serious. You want to be on the look for greater opportunities such as the investment GoPro, the California camera maker that specializes in rugged cameras that can easily be mounted to capture the endeavors of outdoor sports enthusiasts received from Foxconn. Officially known as Hon Hai Precission forked over $200 million for an 8.88% stake in Go Pro. WHEW! You want an investor like this knocking on your door.

The attraction was the seamless growth of GoPro, selling 800,000 cameras with a 300% growth last year. Foxconn was better known for its role as one of Apple's most important Chinese-based manufacturing partners. The company has set its sights on expanding into Brazil, then a rumored US factory where significant robotization of its already successful production lines.

Case #2

At the time of writing, July 3, 2014, Zack (Danger) Brown launched a campaign on Kickstarter to raise money to make potato salad. He offered no business plan or business concept. He laid no claim to success of his potato salad. He wrote, "I'm making potato salad. I haven't decided what kind yet." He asked for ten dollars. By Wednesday afternoon, the same day, he received pledges amounting to more than seventy grand. He followed up by writing "it might not be that good, it's my first potato salad." And the money kept coming in thanks to Brown's sharing on Facebook, Reddit and his other social networks. Many of the donations were in the form of a dollar, or two, or three, but several were in the thousands.

The question remains. Why have so many people donated for potato salad? Depending on your sense of humor, the responses included its odd simplicity, simply funny, best laugh I had in a while, and one donor wrote "I pledged to him, not to receive a photo of the potato salad, but because I love the idea of pledging to a potato salad. It makes me happy when people are not dead serious about everything." Brown chose to give the money away to charity. This taught us an important lesson. Don't take it so serious. You want to enjoy what you do. You want to get up in the morning eager to take on the day and creatively market your products and services to the masses.

How can I have these same investment opportunities?

Back to writing a sponsorship proposal, which could can be a daunting experience. But a big payoff when you deliver. Crafting (10,000–20,000 words) a compelling story with infographics may seem overwhelming when you sit down and look at the first blank page. You must believe in what you have to offer—have a passion for your work—and be ready to put it to paper. Otherwise I suggest you hire a ghostwriter to support your project. Most of my first-time clients come to me because they have a passion, want to grow their business, implement a creative marketing system that includes writing a compelling sponsorship proposal, and don't know where to start. Yes, it is a legitimate process of creating your sponsorship. In fact, most entrepreneurs dissolve their business before really getting started because they have a passion but run out of money.

They did not know how to market their property by seeking sponsorships. Fees for having a sponsorship written by a ghostwriter (who understands sponsorships), range from about $4,000 to over $150,000 for the most respected entrepreneurs.

Writing a compelling sponsorship is something you learn to do. Like the scarcity of natural born brain surgeons there are few natural born writers. You will want to improve your creativity as quickly as possible if you want to receive a high-level sponsorship gift. Sponsors joke that there are 3 keys to writing a compelling sponsorship, and no one seems to know what they are. Here is my approach.

- **Start with what you know and love**

    Don't try to have a passion. When you have a passion the creativity will flow and it will show in your writing.

    As a marketing coach I talk about the importance of understanding your passion and vision. When you find your passion, there is a release in terms of fulfillment, peace, and accomplishment.

    Creating a sponsorship about your passion and what you've already accomplished is where your authenticity will come out. It will give your readers the believability of your story. You will become the expert in your area.

    Many clients ask, *"how do I become an expert in my area?" How do I sell a first-time product or a new sponsorship?* First let me ask you, what is an expert? You don't need to have a PhD or years in formal study in a particular area. If you read three books on any one topic, you're an expert in that topic. That's really what it takes. Someone once said to me "there are no specialists, we are experts."

    I'm not going to diminish the value of having a great deal of knowledge about a particular topic, I don't want you to fret too long about deciding that you are an expert. If you decide you are, then you are. You're ready to move forward.

Decide you're going to be an expert. You know something about something you're interested in. If that's what your business is about - you want to offer an opportunity to a potential sponsor? Then what are you waiting for.

Here is the critical question. *"How do you know sponsors will be interested in your property?"* That's a really good question because it has to be compelling. *"Who is your target market?" "Does anybody really want your property?"* There should be a sense of consumers wanting your property.

If you're offering is about a limited center of interest, such as a family member or a grandpa you really admire, you need to be careful with that offering. That may be an offering of interest to your immediate family, but it may not go beyond that. And potential funders will recognize this fact. I come across sponsorship proposals that are well done, but lack interest to potential funders.

- **Become creative by writing every day.**

It's just like writing a book, it's a skill and it improves with practice. The more you write, the better your chances of improvement. Have dedicated times for your writing—and research.

If your like most entrepreneurs, unless writing is your skill, developing a compelling sponsorship proposal will be challenging. You can't wait for the inspiration to come. This is a horrible way to approach your proposal. You need to have confidence the inspiration will come and assist you while your researching and creating. Otherwise, your potential funders will never know the opportunity you have to offer.

Become your own taskmaster. Commit to a timeline and get your sponsorship proposal completed. This will include making the pre and post phone calls—which we will cover in a later section.

- **Re-write**

  Put your proposal away for a day or two and come back to it. Your initial writing needs to come from the heart. Don't try to correct and look for perfection on your first writing. Just get the first draft down on paper. Each time you look at the proposal you will find ways to improve it with new facts and stories.

- **Read/Research every day.**

  Good storytellers are readers first and foremost. Several years ago, while deciding what I wanted to do with my career, I decided to spend two hours a day reading and listening to positive books. That practice had a dramatic effect on my personal confidence but also gave me focus on what I could offer using my 'expert' advice. If you say you don't have time to read or you don't need to read to write a compelling sponsorship proposal—you're kidding yourself about wanting to take your business to the next level of success.

  Your experience is likely the best place to look for a convincing topic. I encourage first-time sponsorship seekers to come up with a 20-minute live presentation on their property. Volunteer to present the message to local civic groups. Organizations like the Rotary, Kiwanis, Jaycees, and thousands of others, which have weekly meetings and are always looking for interesting topics. This will allow you the opportunity to refine your message and get the feedback of the audience. This is a great format of market research to creating a compelling proposal.

What do sponsors look for?

You may be interested to know what sponsors are looking for. Many have a long history of supporting the public sector and entrepreneurs. So even if you are a marketing whiz you will want to be familiar with all the ins and outs of writing a compelling proposal.

First, be aware that 90% of sponsorship proposals go directly to the marketing executives. Most will have a set of standards and guidelines to follow when making a decision to support or not support your property. From my research marketers will reject nearly 99% of first-time proposals they receive. Of course they look for compelling stories and organizations that are in alignment with their mission and strategic goals for supporting the community and increasing their bottom line. If you're looking for the standard sponsorship proposal, you've come to the wrong place. Each proposal needs to be customized to meet the needs of the sponsor.

Ultimately sponsors are looking for three specific things:

1. A compelling story—this is a given. The message must be fresh and offer a new perspective. There must be a market need and a "hook" to engage the sponsor. While there must be a new element to your property, NEVER tell the decision maker there is "nothing like this" that's ever been done before. That will get you rejected quickly.

2. Clear Premise—do you have a clear premise? Have you identified a need and proposed solution? Have you stated that clearly in 2-3 sentences? A lengthy or unclear premise will tell the decision maker instantly that the proposal will be unclear as well. Think of it this way—a sponsorship proposal is a pre-packaged solution to a problem. Get used to getting to the point quickly. In many proposals writers will spend far too much time telling the sponsor what they are going to talk about.

3. Marketing and reach—this is expected in a proposal. How will you market your sponsor to your client's, network, media etc.? You need to be exceptionally creative when listing your marketing benefits.

No matter how wonderful your knowledge of the content presented, no one will know about you or your property unless you promote and market your work. I have been researching 'how to write' compelling proposals through conversations with corporate decision makers. The most important takeaway I will share is that 90 percent of your success comes from your ability to promote and market your sponsor.

Recognize that there are plenty of wonderful proposals submitted to corporations everyday. Your proposal may represent thousands of hours of research, and take months before you receive a response. What I am telling you is not to put all your resources in one basket. You need to diversify by creating exceptional income by using your property to drive traffic back to your website where you provide a variety of products and services for a cost. Don't sit quietly while hoping for a major sponsor to solve your financial needs.

Writing a compelling sponsorship proposal requires organization and discipline. You must approach it just as you would an ice cream truck business or planning an event. Don't expect a magical moment of inspiration that causes something great to appear. No, I find that great proposals come from productive people. Set aside large blocks of time for creating, whether you feel inspired or not. Practice by writing blogs or newsletters; be intentional. I am intentional with my Monday morning blog posts. This is not always my most inspiration time of the day or week, but I know it's on my calendar as my creative writing time. Once I start researching a topic I type words that come to mind, later the inspiration kicks in and I am able to go back and rewrite with a more compelling story.

BONUS

Keep note pads everywhere—next to your bed, in your car, on the refrigerator, and in the bathroom. When you have a thought about something that would add to the proposal—write it down before you forget. Of course if you're driving you may prefer to use your voice memo on your cell. Most people will lose their best ideas because they say "I'll remember" then lose the thought when they are back to writing their proposal. Become skillful in capturing useful ideas that enter your mind. They will come to you at the most inopportune times.

Can you provide quick tips for creating a compelling sponsor proposal?

We often spin our wheels looking for sponsorships (Partners) for a specific program or event. Let's think about this for a minute. What if you could secure an annual or multi-year sponsorship? Will that work better for you? Then what are you waiting for? Now you get to have some fun. See how many sponsor benefits could you come up with—other than the ones I already shared. Be crazy, outrageous, wild, and have some fun. Perhaps you're looking for funding for your potato salad.

There are times when you may need to provide a sample (standards) and be clear that a customized proposal is created for each sponsor.

I suggest creating at least four (minimum three) levels of sponsorship. Be creative with your sponsor levels. Traditional levels are Gold, Silver, and Bronze. Be creative and name your sponsor levels something that is relevant to your organization. This will be one of the most important pages your sponsor will read.

Use this page to demonstrate your creative marketing strategies and you will captivate your corporate partner.

- What's in it for them? (WIIFM)
- How will you market them?

- What is your audience reach?
- What are your assets?
- What are the benefits to the sponsor?
- What is your call to action?

Captivate Your Sponsor
- List other sponsors - including in-kind and media sponsors.
- Be creative, use your inspiration, your style, and WOW the reader.

How quickly should I begin to look for a corporate partner?

You want to seek corporate partners almost immediately. If you start earning your first dollar early on, you can invest that money back into your business, but if it takes you years before you earn your first dollar you are risking running out of money and losing your business. Avoid the risk of being first with the idea that will become the next great product your customers are looking for.

A corporate sponsor receives dozens of proposals
make yours stand out.

how to secure
a business partner

Y ou received a return call from your potential sponsor (or you got through directly), you've made an appointment with them, and you've shown up (on time) at the person's office or at a neutral meeting spot, like a café. Now that you have the person sitting in front of you and have their full attention, what do you say? You've spent months, hours, and days serving your customers. Now it's time to close the deal. How do you innovate, captivate, and convert your customer?

This is your time to shine. What you say (and don't say), as well as how you guide the conversation, will determine whether you leave empty-handed or with a commitment.

What are some killer opening questions to ask?

A few of my favorite questions to ask at the beginning of a conversation with donors include:

- "Mr. Smith, when I say [insert the name of your organization], what one word comes to mind?"
- "Ms. Jones, what positive things do you see [insert the name of your organization] doing in the community?
- "Mr. Peters, what one thing would you like to see [insert the name of your organization] do for our community?"

Questions like this are designed to get the sponsor's opinion and feedback and to have them feel like they are in control of the conversation. (They really aren't, but we'll get into that in a moment.)

What are some questions never to ask a customer?

A common concept in coaching is that there are no dumb questions. When talking with customers, however, there are some very dumb questions that should never come out of your mouth. They include these:

- "Have you ever heard of [insert the name of your organization]?" (If they say no, then why should they become your customer?)
- "Tell me about your company." (You're approaching them for sponsorship money, so you should know all about them already.)
- "What will it take to get you to partner [insert the name of your organization]?" (This conjures up images of the old, stereotypical used car salesperson. Don't go there.)

Additionally, if you mispronounce the person's name, you're heading for trouble. With all the diversity in today's society, it can be difficult to say someone's name correctly. If you're meeting with someone who has a tricky name to pronounce, practice saying it beforehand.

Do I need to know everything about my organization and how it operates when I talk to a potential sponsor?

If you are the President, CEO, Chief Inspiration Officer, or whatever title you give yourself, YES you should have a good handle on the nuts and bolts of your enterprise. Be cautious, too often people get stuck and think they have to know every single thing about your organization, so they spend hours and hours researching but never research their potential sponsor or ask questions. What if you spend those hours learning about your potential sponsor? Do you think this would give you a foot up on securing a corporate sponsorship?

To raise money for your enterprise, you don't need to know every minute detail. Sure, you need to know where the money is going, what kind of programs | services your enterprise offers, what kind of results they get, how your organization impacts the economic development, and other surface level information. But you don't need to know how the program works minute by minute, who makes what decision day to day, and other nitty-gritty details.

You also need to know if the money given is tax deductible. There are some rules in owning a small to mid-size business concerning taxes. You can find out from your accountant how it works in your area.

TIP: If you secure a charity as a partner a percentage of your corporate sponsorship dollars will be tax-deductible to the corporation.

How do I stay in control of the conversation?

Remember this ole' sales saying: "He who asks the questions controls the conversation." In other words, you need to ask questions of your potential sponsor rather than simply tell them everything you know. If you've been strategic with your creative marketing, this could be a short conversation.

The best entrepreneurs ask questions, lots of them. If you go into your meeting and spend all your time telling the other person how wonderful your business is, that won't get you the results you want. Talk about them.

The key to getting the person or corporation to partner with you is to know what their passions are—their corporate strategies and initiatives, what interests they have in the community and what they want to see happen. The only way to know those things is to ask.

And, yes, it's okay to ask personal questions, as long as you phrase them correctly. For example, suppose you're seeking money for a specific program you provide. The program is an adult learning center and you've heard through the grapevine that the person you're talking with volunteers at the local library teaching ESL (English as a Second Language). Since it's not pubic knowledge, don't say, "Isn't it true that you volunteer at the local library?" That's tacky and obtrusive. Rather, you could ask, "Do you know someone who has a need to be educated in the English language?" The person will likely reveal their personal connection.

If the person you're talking with has a personal story that's been featured in the news, it's okay to relate that to your cause. For example, if you're an attorney and raising money to support your program that fights drunk driving, and the person you're talking with was featured in the news because their son died as a result of a drunk driver, you could say, "We understand that you are fighting to rid the roads of drunk drivers. That's exactly what our organization does. Can we count on your corporate sponsorship?"

The key is to use your questions to lead the conversation and ultimately the sponsor will say "yes" to building a partnership. What questions are you going to ask at your next donor meeting? In the tools section, I will provide a sample sponsorship proposal. It will be up to you to create a compelling proposal using your stories to convert a corporation in to a partner.

make the magic happen and get to the sale

all successful entrepreneurial businesses ultimately come down to the sale, which is nothing more than your asking a customer for what you want. If you never ask, you'll never get. But you don't want to risk asking at the wrong time. You need to do your "ask" at the right moment and in the right way.

Why is it that two restaurants start a business at the same time, in the same geographic area and 50 years later one is a multi-billion dollar business and the other is still a small business? Before answering this question, ask yourself "what do I want my business to look like in fifty years?"

It doesn't matter how you envision your business, it's up to you to create the magic. You always need to be on the lookout for good ideas that will help your business grow in the direction you select.

What is the best time to do "the ask" when speaking with a customer?

I don't close, I ask a customer "are you ready to start growing your business?" Even though "the ask" is akin to "the close" in sales, you don't want to wait until the end of your conversation to bring it up. In fact, the best time to ask is at the beginning of the meeting. In other words, start at the end.

When you're talking one-on-one with a customer, especially someone who doesn't have a lot of time and who knows why you're meeting, you want to respect their time. Often, the person can only spare 10 to 15 minutes with you, so you better get right to the point, or you may miss your chance. Or better yet you can avoid the dreaded ask by implementing a creative marketing system where the customer calls you.

What's the best way to phrase "the ask"?

All questions to your customer, especially your "ask" question, should be open-ended. In other words, don't ask a question that prompts a "yes" or "no" reply. Rather than asking, "Are you ready to make a purchase?" ask "When do you want your items delivered?"

This approach has one main benefit:

1. You're "assuming the sale" and not giving the person a chance to say no.

It takes practice to be direct; customers will respect you more when you get to the point. Of course, they may reply with questions for you, such as:

- "What value will I get from your product | services?"
- "What is your organization doing differently than your competition?"

This is when you go into the details of what your business does—after "the ask." You can talk about how many people your business serves, specific products and services you're offering, success rates for your customers, etc.

What signals do you look for to get commitment from the customer?

When you're talking face-to-face with a customer, always look at the person's body language, as that often gives away more about what the person is thinking than their words.

Are they acting distracted (doodling, tapping their fingers, looking at their phone), as if they'd rather not be there? Is their body "closed" to you (arms crossed)? Or are they engaged and making eye contact? Are they leaning in to talk with you? Reading body language is a skill that you need to practice. After all, someone could have their arms crossed because the room is cold. So look at the whole picture, not just one element, and read all the cues around you to determine how the meeting is really going.

Above all else, don't be afraid to be direct with your ask. Remember the ole' saying, "Ask and you shall receive." Whom are you going to ask today?

overcome rejection

Sometimes, the customer will tell you "no." That's okay, because a "no" doesn't always mean "no." Often, a "no" is a "maybe" or a "tell me more" in disguise. The good news is that you can turn a "no" into a "yes."

What's the best way to turn a "no" into a "yes"?
To begin, make sure you cover all the known objections you routinely hear in your main presentation throughout your social networks. Weave these objections into your blogs and newsletters. Typically, every organization has a few objections they hear over and over. Since you know you're likely to hear those objections, deal with them head-on before the customer has a chance to mention them.

Also, when someone says "no," they typically give a reason, such as, "No. This is not in our budget for this year." If they don't give a reason, ask for one by stating, "What's making you say 'no'?"

When you know the reason behind the "no," you can combat it and turn it into a "yes."

Are there any tools you can recommend to help me develop my objection-countering skills?

I keep (and regularly review) a list of comebacks to objections I often hear from prospective donors. They are disguised in my blogs. I can provide some examples, but you know your donors best. Start listening, and create your catalog of comebacks to overcome objections or rejections from your customer.

Use open-ended and closed-ended questions to your advantage. Know the difference between an open-ended question and a closed-ended one. Open-ended questions could give you valuable information about the customer. Closed-ended questions give you a simple "yes or no" answer. Which would you prefer? If you answered, "It depends on the situation" you are correct!

It's not easy; this application takes practice. I recommend a daily practice of using open-ended questions. Phrase your question in a way that the customer must answer with a feeling or with their intentions for buying. Your questions should start with the "W's"—who, why, what, and how. When you put the "W's" into practice, remember the most valuable rule of thumb: you will gain valuable information about your customer.

Here are samples of open-ended questions:

"I see you have been a customer of [Your organization name here] in the past, what does the business mean to you?"

"Congratulations on being named one of the *Top 50 Women in Business*. What do you feel contributed to your success?"

"I see you buy from [another organization name], what information can I provide you about my organization for you to give?

Here are samples of close-ended questions:

"Would you like a cup of coffee?"

"Will you buy from my organization?"

If you forget and ask a closed-ended question, you can quickly recover by asking a more specific question:

Why do my consumers keep saying "no"?

If you constantly get a "no", you need to do some more questioning—but this time of yourself. Evaluate your approach.

- Are you asking questions?
- Are you asking the *right* questions?
- Are you filling the customer's need?
- Are you personable?
- Would you buy from you?

If you're not sure of your approach or how you come off to others, ask a trusted colleague or friend, and let them know that you don't want a sugarcoated answer. Ask them to be brutal and give you the truth. The more you evaluate your skills and then make positive corrections, the better your bottom line results will be.

From controlling the conversation to giving "the ask" to combating objections to assessing yourself, questions are the key to success. What questions are you going to ask today?

When is the last time you allowed a customer to feel good about themselves?

CHAPTER 14

stay the course

as exotic as everything may sound when using your social networks to serve your customers, don't ignore the ole' fashion methods of marketing. Many of these strategies are still applicable in today's creative marketing system. Don't ignore the obvious. Here are two examples of implementing the ole' school of marketing.

Case Study #1

I was sitting in from of a florist on Valentines Day. They had a wonder display in their window, which read "Show your love today by sending your sweetheart flowers." Ah unfortunately I told my husband years ago don't send me flowers. HE LISTENED! I'm digressing. The florist was located on the corner of a busy intersection. Depending on the color of the light the florist has a captured audience. Immediately I said to myself, I talk to my self a great deal, they should have their telephone number displayed where busy motorist can see their display and be reminded "oh dam I forgot to send my special person flowers." The motorist can immediately pick up their cell, place an order, have the flowers delivered, and be the hero they want to be for their loved one.

After sharing my suggestion with this florist, that was nearly five years ago, their business had tripled by making this little change to their window display. I call this an example of ole' school of marketing.

Case Study #2

My family and I were at the beach. It was a hot August day and we were having lunch on the pier where many of the local shops were located. One of the stores intrigued me. In the doorway stood an employee who, in her softly spoken voice, would say, "come in to our store—everything changes color in the sunlight." Other tourist would pass by smile and continue walking. Nothing was attracting shoppers to enter this store.

I was feeling this young ladies pain. I learned this was her business. She loved crafting and started her business several years earlier selling on Pinterest. She decided through suggestions of others to sell at the beach, a hot spot for tourist. They were correct; selling at the beach was an awesome idea. Her struggle was not inventory her struggle was selling. Apparently she was not comfortable speaking to people and she wasn't giving up on her dream.

She was missing the obvious in her display. If her items would change color in sunlight, she had to change the layout of her store to allow her customers to see the before and after effect. Once she made the change customers were more interested in what she was offering.

Rejection hurts, and giving up is all too easy. When someone says "no" to you, even after you employ the key questions and tactics from

Chapter 10, you have to stay the course. You have to hang in there. Remember, a "no" doesn't always mean "no."

If you immediately quit after someone says "no," that means you don't believe in what you're doing. And if you're going to quit that easily, then you're in the wrong field. You should consider a J.O.B.

The general rule of becoming an entrepreneur is that most customers will buy after the seventh attempt. That means they've said "no" seven times before saying "yes." Why, because there were doing research on your enterprise, your products and services. They were listening to millions of friends on their social media sites. Therefore, you need to be intentional with your marketing strategies and be prepared to intentionally serve your customers over and over again before someone responds favorably. Additionally, when a customer sees that you're hanging in there and are persistent, you'll win them over.

Is there ever a point when you have to throw in the towel?

Of course, you may get to a point when a customer says, "I told you 'no' and that's it!" In this case, you may want to pull back for now, but still follow up with them through social media or on your mailing list.

Or you could nicely say, "Apparently this is not a good time for you. When would you like for me to come back to discuss this?" If they get nasty and yell out, "Never!" then that's your cue to leave. Run…run as fast as you can. It's not worth the fight anymore. But usually, when you're nice and showing consideration for them, they'll tell you to come back next month, next quarter, or next year. There are other fish in the sea. Time to go deep-sea fishing.

I have an intensive list of people who receive my blog | newsletter. Many are close friends, some customers, and others who just want to know what Connie Pheiff is up to these days. I still am surprised when I see people ask to be removed from my mailing list. I don't let this disturb me. I know my programs may not suit everyone and I will work harder to serve my customers.

But I really believe in my product and services. How can I get people to see what I see?

If someone keeps rejecting you and you truly believe in your heart that this is the perfect match for your customer, you could say, "Mr. Redding, I must be doing something wrong because you continue to reject me. I believe that my product and services is the best, and we offer the best value to help you with your problem [name the problem that has already been determined]. Can you help me better understand? What would *you* like to see us do differently?"

When you use this approach, you're going back to them, putting the ownership on them, and allowing them to make decisions.

By considering their input, you're increasing their ego. And by asking and not telling, you're showing them you have a very strong belief and commitment to your organization and to what it does for the community.

Of course, if the person still doesn't see what you see, and if the person is getting agitated by your presence, it may be time to back off— at least for now.

Ultimately, your level of commitment and perseverance is directly related to your belief in your organization. How strong is your belief?

Simple can be harder than complex. You have to work hard to get your thinking clean to make it simple. But it's worth it in the end, because once you get there, you can move mountains.
—Steve Jobs

when customers leave

i t's a fact of business and life that sometimes you'll lose a customer. Yes, it's painful. Yes, it's confusing (especially when they have been a loyal customer for many years), but it does happen. But rather than whine and complain about it (or use it as an excuse not to do better), you need to find out the reason behind it. When you do, not only can you win the customer back, but you can also stop a potential trend from occurring, where a stream of people suddenly stop buying.

Why, specifically, do people stop buying?

That's the question you need to ask your customer. If you are losing customers, you need to find out why, and the best way to do that is to ask, "What is influencing your decision to not buy from us any longer?"

It's a simple question but it can reveal so much. The reasons you uncover can range from something your product did or didn't deliver to something you personally did or didn't do to something internally within the individual or his or her situation. However, you don't know unless you ask.

Do we need to establish a sustainability strategy?

All entrepreneurs need to plan for the unexpected. Let's face it unless you continually change and increase your product and services, your business could perish. Consider today's demographics, the Baby Boomers, are getting older and soon their numbers will start to decline. That will definitely impact the number of customers in today's marketplace. One way to prevent that falloff is to speak with a financial planner to outline your future financial plans. Also, when you have a sustainability plan in place, it can help cushion you when a regular source of income is no longer there, such as when a corporate sponsorship (partner) falls through. You can't put all your eggs in one basket. Counting on one source of income that fails could end your dreams.

I've asked someone why they are no longer buying, and they said that they are disappointed with the organization. How do I handle that?

The best way to handle someone who is disappointed with your programs or services is to ask straightforward questions. Find out specifically what the problem is. Is it something you can personally resolve? If so, then do it. Often, you'll find that someone is mad because of some misinformation they received.

If you find that someone is mad at your business due to reasons you cannot control, take the time to listen to what the person says. Sometimes they just need someone to vent to. For example, one nonprofit I was helping was going through a major reorganization of programs. Many of the volunteers were upset; the reorganization was something I could not control. The organization was making the changes based on key data it had gathered, and it was happening no matter what.

While I couldn't resolve the volunteer's issues with the reorganization, I could hear them out. To do so, I met with the upset volunteer's weekly, kept them current on the progression of the merger through social networks, and just listened to their concerns. I educated them about the reorganization as best as I could. I assured them the new programs would be just as beneficial to the community as the previous ones. And I ultimately had to tell them that the reorganization was happening whether they wanted it to or not.

Some people did stop giving of their time and money completely, but not all did. Some eventually understood and remained committed to the organization and its new direction.

Should you find yourself in a situation where customers are upset at you for something you cannot control, make sure you engage in positive marketing and branding campaign. Serve your customers; keep them informed of your programs and services you offer, how different divisions of the enterprise work together (or how they don't if they're completely separate entities). For example, many people I'm a radio personality, many don't know I am an international speaker and author.

So the bottom line is to deal with leaving and upset customer's head-on. Listen to what they say, and offer either a solution or some education about your products and services. Not everyone is going to be happy with your answer, and that's okay. As long as you're staying focused on the values of your business, you'll persevere through thick and thin. Who are you going to listen to today?

manage your time, or it will manage you

a s an entrepreneur, you have lots of things to do on any given day. We all do. That's why time management is so vital to success. When you can manage your time well, you can get more done in a productive and effective way.

We're all given the same amount of time every day to get our tasks done. So why is it that some people accomplish everything on their to-do list with grace and ease, while others accomplish only a fraction of equally demanding tasks and bemoan the fact that they "have no time"? The secret is not to just manage your time, but also to TAKE CONTROL of it.

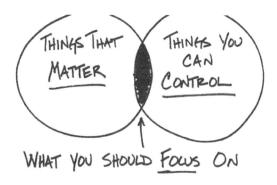

But what if I really don't have enough time?

When you constantly tell yourself, "There's not enough time," guess what? You won't have enough time. How about telling yourself that you do have time?

I went back to school as an adult. I attended full-time, worked full-time, and took care of my family as a single mom. When I completed my classes, I was on the dean's list, and I was excelling at work. Plus, my family still liked me. So when someone says to me, "I don't have enough time," I tell them, "You're full of it. Stop whining."

You do have the time! As I always say, "Wherever you are, whatever you're doing, the time is always the same. The time is now."

If you're not getting something done, you're likely procrastinating. Fortunately, it's never too late to turn around and get things done. For example, my brother recently decided that he wanted to open a restaurant. When I asked him when he was planning on doing it, he said, "I don't know. I'm 45. When am I going to have the time to do it?"

I looked at him and said, "Today! If you want to do it, then do it!"

A few weeks later he opened his restaurant. So again, the time is now. You need to take control of your life. That's the only way to manage it.

How can I get a better handle on my schedule?

Look at what you've been doing over the past few weeks—both professionally and personally. What are you spending your time on? You may say that you have no time, but really look at what you're doing throughout the day.

- Are you spending three hours each night watching TV?
- Are you wasting five hours surfing the web or social media sites?
- Are you not planning your routes for customer visits effectively—constantly zipping back and forth across town or counties rather than clustering your visits?

Really analyze your schedule to see where your time wasting activities are, and then get **RID** of them. Simplify and divide the business tasks where workers can easily be trained.

We can all learn from the hiring and training system of McDonalds. New hires are trained to be expert workers in 20-minutes.

Re-engineering is really the process of optimizing al available resources. Think about the resources you have available that will allow you to maximize your new creative marketing system. Do you have employees that speak another language, or someone that loves to be on Facebook and has embraced social networking? Think bigger; always be on the lookout for opportunities.

Something I learned a long ago was that the best way to control my time and become a better person was to shut the television off. These days I would expand that to include shutting off social media sites, unless I'm using it to follow customers, offer a service, and learn new information about a customer, posting blogs, or responding to someone's else's blog, which is very intentional. Get rid of the distractions that take you away from what you really want to do. That's the best way to get a handle on your time.

Controlling your time is a choice. What choices are you going to make today to ensure you have enough time to get it all done?

the 4 biggest mistakes an entrepreneur makes

We all make mistakes. There's no shame in that. But are you learning from your mistakes? Are you picking yourself up and changing course, so you don't make the same mistake again?

When it comes to running your own business, there are four main mistakes I see entrepreneurs make. Beware of them, and know how to fix them, so they don't derail your efforts or your passion.

Mistake #1: Getting into a business for the wrong reasons.
If you don't love what you do, if you don't have a passion for your work, your success is going to be a long and hard road. Unfortunately, I've seen some people get into business because they view it as just

another hobby. Or they've been downsized and thought since the job market is lousy I'll hang a shingle on my garage and start a business without any planning.

I can sell anything, they think. You may be a great salesperson, but if you don't truly believe in your passion and your products and services, you'll have a hard time getting people to purchase your stuff. Plain and simple!

Mistake #2: Not realizing that your attitude controls your success.

Are you genuinely happy to be doing what you do? Do you believe in yourself and your passion? Do you view the world in a positive or negative light? Your answers to these types of questions will determine your attitude, and your attitude determines your success.

The people you speak to every day, whether via phone or in person, can pick up on your true attitude, regardless of the actual words you use. You know this is true, because you do it to others, too. For example, you've likely gone into a retail store to purchase something and have had to interact with salespeople who would rather not be there that day. Even if the salesperson answers all your questions and rings up your transaction quickly, you can sense if the person cares or is just there to collect a paycheck.

Your customers can sense the same thing in you! So make sure your attitude is one that customers will want to interact with.

Mistake #3: Continually blaming other people or events for your failures.

It's very easy (and very tempting) to blame others for our failures. But at the end of the day, the only thing that really determines your success is you.

Blaming others is nothing more than excuse- making. How many times have you heard someone say (or have you said), "I didn't sell anything today because …

- I didn't have a new brochure to give out.
- My contact didn't give me a proper referral.
- The economy is really bad.
- I heard that people aren't buying what they used to.
- I couldn't get online today.

The list of excuses and blaming is endless.

Here's the truth: If you're in the right job and have the right attitude, there's no need to blame anyone or anything else. You can sell without a brochure, without a proper referral, and without a booming economy. Entrepreneurs still bring in the big money; you just have to approach it wisely.

Mistake #4: Trying to sell the products rather than getting people to want to buy your products.

Always remember that you're selling your passion, whether it's a product or service. So you can't "sell" the organization. Your role is to show customers the value of your products and services. People buy when they believe in what you have to offer. You gain that belief by asking questions, uncovering their passions, and showing how the products and services align with the person's interests. Attitude and passion are what generate sales, not fancy salesmanship.

INNOVATE + CAPTIVATE = CONVERT

No matter what mistakes you've made in the past, you can overcome them and change your approach. Which of these mistakes have you made in the past? How are you going to change your approach so you don't make them again?

READY, SET, GROW YOUR MARKET

stand out
from the crowd

C hances are customers you're approaching are also being approached by your competition. After all, the other organizations have the same database you do. Whether you're a small entrepreneur or large national corporation, how do you set yourself apart?

> *Don't do things better, do things differently.*
> **—Steve Jobs**

Since most entrepreneurial businesses have a small certain percentage of their budget earmarked for marketing, you need to implement a creative marketing system where you will stand out in the eyes of your customers.

Example: Statistics show (source unknown) that customers will buy from a business that supports their charity. Many retail outlets do this well. They select a day of the week and market for each dollar sold the retail will give to their charity. Consumers are savvy and looking for unique ways to support the community. Stand out and allow a consumer to think of your business first. It's a tall order, indeed, but it can be done! Through my business I partner with Dress for Success and the national Foundation Center. At the end of the year each receive percentage of my book sales. It's a win-win proposition. I like to place this strategy in the category of creative marketing.

How do I stand out from all the other entrepreneurs with the same offerings?

In order to stand out, you need to focus on three key things: Credibility, Consistency, and Follow- Up.

- When you're **credible**, people believe that you'll do what you say you'll do. They see you as someone of your word and are eager to do business with you. You develop credibility by being honest, trustworthy, and transparent. You don't hide details, and you "tell it like it is" in a tactful way.
- To be **consistent** means that the image you put out is the real you, 100% of the time. You're not putting out the image of a business professional and then dancing on the tables at bars on the weekends. Of course, a lack of consistency doesn't have to be that extreme. Someone once paid me a great compliment. They said, "You make every person you meet feel like the greatest person in the world and your best friend." Now realize that I'm not a "hugger" or overly friendly. But when I run into people on

the street, I stop and chat with them. I ask how they are (without asking for a sale). In other words, I consistently work on the relationship even when I'm not formally meeting with them. By being consistent like this, I develop strong relationships with customers, making it easier to ask them for a sale later on. They know that I care about them and not just their business.

- We've talked about **follow-up** in a previous chapter, but it's worth mentioning again. You can't just talk with your customers when you're asking for a sale. You want to make sure you're following up with them and "touching" them throughout the year. For example they're getting honored for something in your community try to attend the ceremony. If you learned that they just had a baby, send a congratulations card. If you saw them written up in the newspaper (for something positive), write a note telling them how great it was to read about their project or initiative or whatever the article was about. Follow-up shows that you're aware of what they're doing and taking an interest in them.

How do I create a personal brand for myself?

The best entrepreneurs not only stand tall, they shine bright creating a personal brand. Just as corporations have a brand, entrepreneurs and people have brands, too. It's what they're known for and how they present themselves in the marketplace.

For example, when my customers think of me, they immediately think of someone who is prepared, who has character, has a passion for life, and is a marketing and social media strategist. That's part of my brand—what I'm known for. When someone meets with me, they know that I've done my research. I already know whether the customer I'm meeting is a fit for my work. Whether through actual research or good questioning during casual meetings and networking functions, I am prepared and ready to ask for the sale — through creative marketing of course!

The key to creating a personal brand is to figure out how you can present yourself different than other entrepreneurs. Often, this means stepping up your game and becoming a better communicator. It's about being excited about what you're doing. It's about asking good questions to learn more about your customer and demographic needs.

So what can you do that's different or exceptional to set yourself apart? What can you become known for in your niche? Being like everyone else is the not the key to success; rather, it's about setting yourself apart and being known for something great. Steve Jobs is a great example of setting creative marketing—building a brand that is different than his competition. There are many companies that sell computers. Apple sells an image. It's status to own an Apple product.

I know it's difficult to gather the courage to break from the pack. For many years of my life, I always felt like a square peg trying to fit into a round hole. I never felt like I fit, although I tried very hard to, and I struggled with that. It was only when I gave myself permission to embrace who I was, to be confident being the one doing things different, that I started seeing what was possible.

You want to be that one person who stands out, who is doing it different, who has a compelling brand. When you can do that, customers will welcome you with open arms.

What's the guru's secret to really standing out?

I've mentioned this before, and depending on your business model, my favorite way to stand out is to send people handwritten notes. Or a quick text to let your regular customers know "for a limited time, we have a special" or "your favorite product or

service is available for a short time." Allow your customer to feel special, wanted, and appreciated by you.

Let me say it again: handwritten notes, handwritten notes, handwritten notes. Did I mention handwritten notes? But this is only the cherry on top. Before sending the note I become the guru in my niche by owning my brand, by having credibility to market with ethics, and by bringing value to my customers. In other words, I live by the advice I outline in this book, and I personally do everything I recommend that you do.

When it comes time to send the handwritten notes, I have something personalized and meaningful to write in each, and I actually write them myself. This will take time, but it's worth every minute. I know there are services out there that will send cards on your behalf, and they make the font appear like handwriting. I'm not comfortable with that because you never know what the end product looks like. Plus, even though the font resembles handwriting, it's not my handwriting. People receiving the card still know it's a computer font. That's why I prefer the good, old-fashioned handwritten note. Event planners love when they receive my notes. How do I know this, they tell me.

You can buy blank Thank You cards at any discount store or card shop. Or you can opt for custom cards that have your name printed on them. You can even use stationery in lieu of a card. It's up to you. The key is actually writing out the note yourself in longhand. That's what really makes you stand out.

Apparently, I'm not the only successful entrepreneur that employs this technique. One of my former neighbors ran one of the biggest foundations in the country. Every morning I would see him on his back porch reading the newspaper. I'd often say "Hi," and on occasion even ask if he'd like to join me for coffee or a morning run (since we were both up so early), and he always replied "no." He said that he needed to spend that early morning time reading the paper.

Eventually, I asked him why he was so committed to reading the paper each day. He said, "I read the obituaries. I read the birth and wedding announcements, I read about who is being honored, and even about who is ill. Every single one of those people gets a handwritten card from me. I've been doing this every day for many years, and this is why my foundation has one of the biggest giving dollars in the country— because I touch them every day."

I admit, I don't go to the extreme that he does, but I do believe in the power of handwritten notes and attribute my success to the practice of sending them. So take some time to look through your customer contacts today. Are they all seeing you as someone credible, consistent, and dedicated to follow-up? Are they receiving handwritten notes from you? Whom are you going to send a card to today? How are you going to truly stand out from the crowd?

deliver an excellent customer service experience

i f you want to be competitive in today's ever-changing global marketplace, you need to deliver a distinctive emotional and personal customer experience. Create an experience that is part of your culture by creating a strong bond with your customer. Customer service is when you go above and beyond your promise. A business that does not embrace service first will most likely lose business. A customer's perception whether positive or negative, is what they will share with their friends.

How do I demonstrate and create a distinct advantage over my competition?

Your goal is to turn consumers into customers, relationships into partnerships, ideas into reality. Here are several key elements I promote when coaching my clients to deliver an excellent customer service experience.

Significance

Who is your customer's first point of contact? One of the most important elements for delivering excellent customer service experience is training your people. Are your people trained on your product features, pricing, or warranties? There is nothing more frustrating than to ask these questions and be told, "I don't know." A business needs to create a seamless customer service experience. Your customer service team needs to be as knowledgeable and efficient as your sales team, and you.

Accessibility

I'll admit the rules for accessibility are changing as rapidly as technology changes. Accessibility is greater today than in past years. Your customers are expecting immediate satisfaction. They know we work with cell phones and have immediate access to telephone calls or emails. If you're unable to respond immediately, develop a system where experienced people can answer the calls.

Functionality

We can all agree cable companies are predictable for providing poor service. I also know of many people who have difficulty when calling their telephone provider (no names). When customers have problems with your products or service you want to provide an excellent process for resolving the problem promptly. If the problem cannot be solved immediately provide your customer a date and time for a follow up call and stick to your promise!

Considerations

The best customer service comes from bartenders. If you think about it excellent customer service requires excellent communication skills and effective listening. Before jumping to conclusions listen to your customer's needs. Excellent communication skills could increase sales. Rather than assuming what the customer wants, learn what the customer needs. You will be creating an emotional connection.

Prevention | solutions

Periodically check in with your customers. Customer service satisfaction surveys can easily be conducted online. When I speak I will ask the event planners and select members of the audience to provide feedback. The only way to know how to serve your customers better is to know their needs. Feedback will also help you increase the value of your products and services.

Creating positive touch points of connection with your customer creates a strong foundation for the ultimate service outcome—*Customer Loyalty.*

What other tools should I look for?

For any entrepreneurial business, people are the organization's most precious resource. When the wrong people are taking on the marketing role, the results can be damaging to your business. Having your best and brightest create the marketing strategies is great, but you also need an individual ready to accept the ole ways and embrace new strategies. Then everyone wins.

Now, let's face reality. An organization with successful campaigns can say they have a robust staff, each person with independent responsibilities and a focus on an area of expertise. But we know that an entrepreneurial organization is not always so fortunate. All too often, we must rely on committed employees with little or no marketing experience. Add in the

Pareto Principle (or the 80/20 rule) where you have 20% of the people doing 80% of the work, and you can see how difficult it can be for a business to thrive from this principle.

In fact, in many businesses, it's common for an employee or you the business owner, to wear the hat of multiple positions. For example, I was once hired as the Executive Director for a local United Way. My background is that of fundraising and leadership. Before long I learned the board had a different plan for me: they also wanted me to be the bookkeeper. I quickly expressed my concerns, because bookkeeping is not one of my strengths. Because of funding, the board could not hire a bookkeeper, so it became me. And I admit it…bookkeeping is not something I enjoy or look forward to doing every day.

Now I'm a business owner, an entrepreneur trying to wear multiple hats. I learned very early in my business it's best to outsource. It has been freeing and I focus on my strengths to build the business. I strongly recommend that if you are wearing multiple hats, be sure all those hats consist of a job you know and are capable of doing. Otherwise you will go bonkers! Outsourcing is a tool I strongly recommend.

Know Your Team

Creative Marketing efforts will have multiple individuals involved, including:

- You. In addition to oversight of your mission and deliverables, you have the responsibility of being the "face of the community."
- Marketing officer. If you are lucky to have a marketing officer, congratulations. A good marketing officer will have good writing and verbal communication skills.
- All staff members. The person leading the marketing efforts needs to keep everyone in the organization up-to-date on the initiatives. Why? You may have a person or team in charge

of the marketing strategies, but when you're an entrepreneur *everyone in the organization is responsible for marketing.* This is a joint effort, period!

- Outside coach. (I recommend having one). If you elect to hire a coach, it is important that the paid staff understand how to surrender control. Yes, this has been an issue. A coach can help you design the marketing plan, address board concerns, lead retreats and training of the plan, and create grassroots efforts where your business and board can work together toward a successful goal. Coaching will develop you and your team into a successful engine for the enterprise. You can find a coach that will help you develop and implement a creative marketing system. For more ideas go to www.idealist.org.

develop
customer loyalty

We would all love to have a loyal following of customers who buy our products and services time and time again. The question is how do you develop that following? Quite simply, you earn it!

Loyalty comes when customers know, like, and respect you. But that doesn't happen overnight. It takes time and consistency to earn customer loyalty. Once you earn it, though, treat it like gold.

Economically, the best strategy for your business is to pursue the creation and sustainability of loyal customers. Your strategic initiative will separate your business from your competition. It has been proven a business with high levels of loyal customers will typically grow their revenue twice the rate of their competition. Your strategy of developing loyal customers needs to be part of your business culture. Which drives the behavior of the people who support your business.

"Quality in a product or service is not what you put into it.
It is what the client or customer gets out of it."
—**Peter Drucker**

As yourself, "what does your customer really want?" What's your definition of customer loyalty? Customer loyalty is different than customer service.

You have a competitive advantage when you develop loyal customers. As an entrepreneur and business leader you have a goal to build a successful and sustainable business. For this to happen you will have many balls in the air and when you are able to manage these four components succinctly, your business will GROW your market.

- Manage the business effectively
- Change, Sustain, and !nnovate
- Create financial growth
- Develop and sustain a loyal customer base.

Loyal customers will always return to purchase your products or services. This is creating a long-term stream of income. It doesn't matter what industry you are in, creating multiple and consistent streams of income will have a positive effect on your business.

Another benefit of developing loyal customers is they will talk about you, boast about your products | services. This is the best creative marketing system yet. Nothing says, "buy my products" better than *word-of-mouth advertising.*

We talked earlier about how consumers are smarter and deepening their understanding before making a purchase. Most likely doing their homework by asking their friends on their social networking sites. Use this to your advantage, not only must you serve your customers, write about your customers, and help them find a restaurant—you must also be prepared for their referrals - because they are talking about you!

For example, would you buy based on an advertisement you seen on a billboard or would you buy based on a referral from someone you know and trust? How did you choose your current dentist, physician, or plumber? Was it a random pick from the yellow pages, or did you ask someone in your network? We typically make our selections based on trusted recommendations. The best referrals are customer referrals.

Okay, so how do I *earn* loyalty?

The more you show customers the value your organization brings to them, the more loyal they'll be to you. This means you're out talking with them about your enterprise throughout the year, not just at the time of asking. You're involved with them continuously. You know what's going on, and you acknowledge them regularly.

You need to show your customer's that you and your business are loyal to them! In other words, loyalty is a two-way street. For example, if your customer runs a printing company, are you using their services for your printing needs (assuming they give you a good price)? If they can't give you the best pricing, are you using a printer in your market?

It's as easy or difficult, for a small business to find one large customer that will buy in bulk. Study your market and find the one benefit you could offer your customer. I'm not talking about making a trade, that doesn't put money in your bank account. I'm saying to be willing to refer your customers to other business that will serve your customers needs. Does it make sense when your customer calls to ask where they get a good dinner in New York City? When you're a printer located in Des Moines? Yes, you are providing a service. They will remember you! I guarantee it. You can easily implement this strategy in your creative marketing system. Consider the story I shared about how Hilton helps their customer by offering services of their competition.

Creating loyalty is a win-win proposition. It's about giving fair value back and forth. That's how you gain loyalty from your customers, so they keep buying from your business.

Is earning loyalty really about being friendly?

I often say that building loyal customers is really friend-raising. It's about establishing good relationships with your customers, because that's what builds loyalty. In fact, the friendlier you are, the more business you'll receive.

So treat everyone as a friend. Call upon your friends when you need help reaching someone. In return, let them know they can call upon you when they need assistance with something, and then give your assistance however you can. If you have a friendly relationship with your customer, it'll build loyalty and attract more friendly relationships to you.

My syndicated radio show *Marketing Masters* guest schedule is packed-full of high-level talent where we talk about their creative marketing strategies for building customer loyalty. This platform allows me to build customer loyalty (friend-raising) by asking my customers to be a guest on the show. Do you think my guest will make recommendations to other A-lister guest? YES, they do! Do you think this will increase my sponsorship levels? Yes, it does!

Realize, too, that this friendly feeling needs to permeate every aspect of your business. That means you have to work to instill a culture of a friendly atmosphere in the workplace. When you have a friendly environment, your customers can see it and sense it. Likewise, if the organization is filled with conflict, customers can see and sense that as well. If there's friction in your organization, bring in a coach to help facilitate resolving the issue.

Always be sure your organization is filled with friendly, helpful people who are dedicated to the mission of your business. And remember, the way you behave and the attitude you exude is exactly how others will respond to you.

Fortunately, creating a friendly environment for yourself and for other people around you doesn't cost a lot, but it does pay off handsomely. How can you expand your circle of loyal customers?

CHAPTER 21

finding
new customers

having a large pool of existing customers you can call upon year after year is great. But at some point you're going to need to attract new customers to your business. In fact, to keep your organization healthy and strong, you'll need a large pipeline of prospective customers you can build friend-raising.

The best way to attract new customers is to go out and look for them. And the best place to start is at local or national networking events. Of course, formal networking is just one tool to expand your reach. You've probably learned or tried many other options, such as getting referrals from current customers or maybe even doing a public speaking event. Those are great too. Your social networks is the easiest way to get in front of lots of people so you can spread your message and meet new potential customers.

Here's a thought! You can license your product | services. You can refer to this team as your affiliates, team, franchise, etc. Only you can decide how to develop this program. When you have affiliates it's a win-win for both your business and your affiliate. They are finding new customers and increasing your brand.

How do I embrace globalization?

You may want to avoid globalization. You can't. Globalization will not avoid you. Are you familiar with the book The World if Flat (Friedman, T., 2005)? Give it a read? Friedman shares how you can turn globalization into an opportunity if you take action.

From the Back Cover

- One mark of a great book is that it makes you see things in a new way, and Mr. Friedman certainly succeeds in that goal," the Nobel laureate Joseph E. Stiglitz wrote in *The New York Times*, reviewing *The World Is Flat* in 2005. For this updated and expanded edition, Friedman has seen his own book in a new way, bringing fresh stories and insights to help us understand the flattening of the world. New material includes:
- The reasons why the flattening of the world "will be seen in time as one of those fundamental shifts or inflection points, like Gutenberg's invention of the printing press, the rise of the nation-state, or the Industrial Revolution"
- An explanation of "uploading" as one of the ten forces that are flattening the world, as blogging, open-source software, pooled knowledge projects like Wikipedia, and podcasting enable individuals to bring their experiences and opinions to the whole world

- A mapping of the New Middle—the places and spaces in the flat world where middle-class jobs will be found—and portraits of the character types who will find success as New Middlers
- An account of the qualities American parents and teachers need to cultivate in young people so that they will be able to thrive in the flat world
- A call for a government-led "geo-green" strategy to preserve the environment and natural resources
- An account of the "globalization of the local": how the flattening of the world is actually strengthening local and regional identities rather than homogenizing the world

But I'm a busy entrepreneur. Do I really have to network?

Many people in business for themselves mistakenly believe that all those networking events they hear about aren't suited for them. They think those events are only beneficial to people in the corporate world looking for sales leads, new vendors, or alliance partners. Nothing could be further from the truth! You're in business for yourself; you need as many sales leads as possible. The trick is to network smartly and develop creative marketing strategies using some of the ole' time-tested methods and include new methods of getting a customer to call you.

Here is my suggestion, select two-three organizations you can put your heart and soul into. I've mentioned that Dress for Success is a charitable partner. I offer my speaking and coaching services to their clients. I'm invited to different networking events in different communities across the country. You can be on the invite list as well and you want to attend those functions! All entrepreneurs need to be networking because the guest just may be your next big client.

Depending on your niche you will want to attend training programs. I am a member of the National Speakers Association nationally and locally. I make it a point to attend my local chapter meeting each month. More importantly I attend the annual conference. It's about learning and the people you meet. Good ole' fashion marketing.

When you attend the various networking events, be friendly, outgoing, and inquisitive. Find out about other attendees and let others know about you. Volunteer to help on different committees. Become a mentor—it will teach you as much as you teach your mentee. Don't start a conversation by spilling your guts telling others about your business. Ask about them first, some good questions to ask your new contact are these:

- What do you do for a living?
- Tell me about your company or what you do in the community?
- What is your organization's mission or vision?
- What kinds of things in the community are important to you or your organization?
- What are you looking for when hiring a keynote speaker?
- Do you work with a business coach?
- How's the family?

Really get to know the person and more about the organization they work for. There is a bank executive I've known for over ten years. Each time I meet with him he ask about the family. He doesn't say bank with us, he wants to know about me. This is a great strategy.

But make sure you don't spend all your time with one person. In fact, if you're timid about networking, here's my advice for making the most of the networking event. When you go to these networking events, put 20 of your business cards in your left pocket. By the time you leave the event, you want your left pocket empty, and you want to have 20 new business cards from the new people you've met in your right pocket.

TIP: You are going to find today's new generation of entrepreneurs without business cards. Be prepared to quickly pull out your cell and type in their information. They will be offering to do the same with you.

Immediately following the event, send each person you met a handwritten note. It can be short and sweet, such as, "It was great meeting you. I learned a lot about your business. I'd love to learn more. Let's have coffee. Tell me when you're available, and we'll set it up."

How much networking do I really have to do?

Most successful entrepreneurs spend approximately 60 to 70 percent of their time networking, doing research, and meeting with potential and current sponsors. Therefore, I suggest you create a weekly plan that allocates a certain number of hours to key activities.

Successful entrepreneurs are busy meeting new customers, promoting the business through radio interviews, networking events, curating funding and hiring a team for the research and development of your products and services. You need to be the face of the organization.

For example, you may decide to devote 12 hours to networking, 12 hours to meeting with prospective and current investors, and 6 hours to research. The remaining 10 hours of your week (assuming a 40-hour workweek) are for "other" office duties you must attend to.

Think of social networking like a game. You want multiple balls in the air. Then, when it comes time to sell your products and services, you catch one ball at a time. The more balls you have in the air, the easier it is to reach your goals because you're not scrambling to find the customers you need. You've already made the connections through your activities; now it's simply time to win the game.

Should I get testimonials from loyal customers to attract new ones?

This is important enough I wanted to repeat. Testimonials are a great way to attract new customers and get them excited about working with you. I have to admit that when I first established my business, I was hesitant to ask for testimonials because I didn't fully understand how powerful they could be. Today, I couldn't imagine being successful without them.

> *Connie's one-on-one coaching has been invaluable in getting my business off the ground. Business planning and marketing are second nature to this pro, she thinks of everything! Connie feels like my partner and to a new entrepreneur, this is very comforting. She gives so much of herself, is very supportive and has an amazing interest in my success. Thank you Connie, I couldn't have done it without you.* ☺
> **—Virginia Becker**
> *electronic pet assistance directory (e-p.a.d)*

When entrepreneurs first hear about the idea of asking loyal customers for a personal testimonial, they often say, "Why do I need one? What would some personal testimonials do for me?" This was the best "I don't need testimonials, my expertise speaks for itself."

When one of my clients said "why do I need a testimonial? My expertise speaks for itself." I have to disagree unless you're Steve Jobs. Could you imagine someone asking "Mr. Jobs, before I agree to work with you I would need to see a testimonial?" That would never happen. So until you get to the level of some of the great entrepreneurs, I suggest you ask for testimonials.

Testimonials from loyal customers build your credibility. When you meet with prospective customers, you need to build credibility and rapport. Sharing some glowing testimonials from others (even people they may know) helps you do that.

For most people, our biggest mistake is not having the courage to talk about ourselves or promote ourselves. It's easy to see why. As children, we're often taught not to brag, sit in the corner, don't speak unless spoken to—sound familiar? But promoting yourself is not bragging. It's simply showing others how you can help them. And it's perfectly okay to do that. In fact, people want that!

If tooting your own horn is difficult for you, testimonials make it easier. With a testimonial from others, you're not saying how wonderful you are; someone else is (and that gives the words more credibility too). So definitely get some testimonials they'll make your marketing efforts so much easier.

What's the best way to ask for a testimonial?

Before you ask for a testimonial, you have to earn it. You can't ask someone to write one for you if you're in the beginning stages of your working relationship. It's almost like a report card, so you have to have a track record with the individual and organization.

If you have established a history with the person—the next time you meet with him or her, say, "Ms. Peterson, I'm so glad you're happy with the work I'm providing and our relationship over the years. I'd be thrilled if you would write a short testimonial about me and how we've worked together so that I can share it with others."

Most often the person is happy to take on the request. Sometimes they'll even ask you to write what you'd like them to say, and then they'll review, make any needed changes, sign their name to it, and put it on their letterhead. When this happens, gladly oblige. Focus the testimonial on what you want to highlight: your leadership skills, marketing ability, work with key groups of people, etc.

When you have a potential new customer, a testimonial is one of the best documents you can provide to assure them there's no risk in working with you or supporting your enterprise. You're showing that you're a reputable professional who is respected by your clients. And what prospective customer wouldn't want to work with someone like that?

assess yourself

n o matter how successful you are working in or on your business, you need to regularly assess your attitude, your skills, and your level of happiness in your chosen business. Why? Because if you could make a few simple changes and be better at what you do, wouldn't you want to know what those few simple changes are? Self-assessment is what makes that possible.

How do I assess my attitude?

Great entrepreneurs are there to help, so that has to be the attitude you embrace—that you're helping the community and helping solve your customer's problems. If your attitude is only that you're in business to raise dollars, then that's not going to work.

What's your attitude right now? If you're unsure whether "helping" is naturally within your nature (it's not for many people, so don't feel bad), I suggest you take a formal self-assessment, such as the DiSC® Type Indicator, to help you determine if your leading a passion or following your passion. It you have a lousy attitude perhaps something should change.

Aside from that, to get an accurate picture of the attitude you're portraying, ask your colleagues, friends, and family. Do they see you as truly helpful or just as someone else asking for money?

Also, ask yourself how you think others perceive you. Do you think you should work on your attitude? (Hint: There is always room for improvement.) So what's your game plan to work on your attitude? What are your goals for this aspect of your self-development?

Look at other successful entrepreneurs: Ben Franklin, Henry Ford, John D. Rockefeller, David Sarnoff, Oprah Winfrey, Steve Jobs, Bill Gates, Thomas Edison, Estee Lauder, Milton Hershey, Ray Kroc, Arthur Davidson, Sam Walton. This is just a short list. You can find many more of the greats on the World Wide Web. What do you admire about them? What don't you admire about them? What attributes of theirs can you develop in yourself?

Consider joining two or three Associations; one association for enhancing your craft, and two others for networking opportunities. Think outside the box when you look to join. Look for a group where you have an interest, but different from what your enterprise offers. These groups will give you some great insights and a great opportunity for implementing your creative marketing strategies. They also offer many programs on personal development throughout the year.

When it comes to personal development and attitude enhancing, I suggest the following key activities:

- Read a positive message every day.
- Do positive affirmations every morning when you wake up.
- Spend at least fifteen minutes a day with your affirmations and reading positive material.
- Surround yourself with positive and motivational images. My motivational picture, my "why," is to live on the beach, So I have a beautiful beach picture complete with palm trees on my phone, on my wall in my office, and as my screensaver on my computer. That's what I desire to go to, so it's visualization.
- Read business books and magazines. There are plenty online.
- Read personal development books. See my recommended reading list at the end of this book.
- Read books about marketing and creativity.
- Attend at least three programs or seminars a year. The topics can range from self-help to business to personal interest. The point is to help make you a well-rounded person.
- Listen to books on CD while in your car. Again, the topics can be anything that interests you and stretches your mind.

The more you feed your mind positive and engaging materials, the better your attitude will be.

How do I assess my business skills?

There's no one right way build your business. It's really about knowing your personal style and what works best for you. However, having said that, there are some specific skills you should evaluate to ensure that you're incorporating them into your business model.

- Are you quick on your feet when you're meeting with a potential customer? You never know what direction the conversation is going to go, so you always need to be prepared for the "what ifs." This includes being prepared for objections, knowing how to handle customers who are upset, and any other what-if scenario that could happen.

- Are your speaking skills finely honed? Since you're talking almost all day to customers and investors, you want to have great speaking skills. If you mumble, use slang, say "um" every other word, or speak in a monotone, few people will want to spend much time with you. Therefore, to assess your speaking skills, record yourself reading a book aloud.

  Also, record yourself during a presentation with a loyal customer. (Ask if they mind first.) Most smart phones have a recording app. If yours does not, you can purchase a low-cost, small digital recorder. After you've recorded yourself, listen to the recordings. Do you like what you hear? Would you want to listen to you? Take a public speaking seminar; join Toastmasters, or the National Speakers Association if you feel you need to improve your communication skills.

- Are you attending regular skills training? Ideally, you should be spending 30 minutes a week in training with your colleagues or with other individuals in your community. By doing this weekly, you'll be able to keep on top of trends and be at the top of your game.

How do I assess my level of happiness?

Confucius said, "Choose a job you love, and you will never have to work a day in your life." Do you love fundraising? Do you have a passion for your work? Do you love meeting people? If you've answered "no" to any of these questions, you may need to re-evaluate whether business ownership is for you.

Today, entrepreneurs are much smarter. They know the enterprise has to run like a well-oiled machine and have the right people doing the right job in order for the business to be successful. If you're not happy, you're not only hurting yourself; you're also hurting others.

That's why you need to answer these questions honestly: "Do I love what I do? Do I have a passion for my work? Am I helping solve my customer's problems?"

It takes a lot of pride to acknowledge any unhappiness due to being in the wrong line of work. Fortunately, if you've been a loyal employee and downsized, chances are your attitude could be a bit jaded. Ultimately, if you hate what you're doing and are unhappy, you owe it to yourself to change course. If you were downsized, like I was, consider it a gift to re-examine your life journey.

Remember, you may be in business for yourself, it isn't like a team sport. You're not competing with anyone. You're only competing with yourself. That's why you need to be your personal best. So, if your business dollars are low, you need to do an internal evaluation: "Am I happy? Am I in the right place? Am I implementing creative marketing strategies to build my business?"

There's no shame in admitting you're in the wrong place. Being an entrepreneur isn't for everyone. It takes a certain kind of person to excel. If you're that person—then great! If not, find what you love.

Realize, too, this does not mean you'll never have a bad day when you question why you're doing what you do. You will have those days. We all do. But every day shouldn't be a bad day.

If you love what you do, you have a passion, and have the ability to make an income through your passion it'll be easy for you to put your whole heart into it.

Winston Churchill once said, "You make a living by what you get. You make a life by what you give." I hope this book has given you the jumpstart you need to put your heart into building your business, your brand, and your passion so you can make the most of this wonderful profession.

Now the power is in your hands. It's time for YOU to get into the groove and develop your creative marketing strategies. By increasing your customer list, raising investor dollars, and securing partners through corporate sponsorships. You have a product or service the world needs. It's up to you to let them know you can solve their problems. Your passion really can change the world.

sample letters & telephone scripts

We need to go deeper. What do you want to project about your business? As entrepreneurs we get too busy, too close, and loose site of our clarity. When you are developing your creative marketing system be certain to package and project your vision for your business. How you impact your customers, and how will you stand out and shine bright and get noticed. The tools I am providing you in this book are drop-dead creative marketing strategies.

Over the last 8 years—I've spent my time as an international speaker, traveling the world talking about creative marketing strategies and executive coaching. I have the opportunity to meet a lot of great people. Over those years I learned skills and experience are not good enough to be different. You get different when you stand out from others and shine bright—become more visible and have a greater impact with your brand and above all have fun.

I didn't get here without creating a marketing system of my own that I follow intentionally. I started with the ole' school of knocking on doors (literally) and mailing flyers. Lets call the following pages the ole' way of creative marketing. These samples may be the ole' way of marketing, but many are still applicable today. All you need to do is personalize the letters and scripts and off you go.

Did you Say "Sponsorship?"

Here are the meat and potatoes of the business tool chest for developing your creative marketing system. Many entrepreneurs can't believe they can secure a corporate sponsorship. They believe sponsorships are for charities. This is true, but entrepreneurs can also capture a piece of the pie. I am sharing with you my full out creative marketing system for securing corporate sponsors—or the official tag is *Business Partner*.

A true sponsorship is a win-win for the corporation and your entrepreneurial business. A true sponsorship is a business or individual giving money for something in return, such as marketing, tickets to an event, or an orchestrated meeting with a VIP, etc. It's up to you and your business to determine what is in it for the sponsor. Another term for exchange of goods and services is "in-kind." In-kind gifts typically come from the media outlets; radio, television, billboards, newspaper, etc. Your business will determine the culture and proper lingo for sponsorships. My goal is to provide you the tools to get Ready, Set, GROW your market.

Where do I start?

I hear from lots of entrepreneurs who would like to create a sustainable organization. Is it possible? Yes. Is it easy? No. But that doesn't need to stop you from doing what you love to do. I have been writing sponsorship proposals for many years, starting with a simple proposal to local businesses to sponsor a luncheon. After several years I began to find a receptive audience for my mission and programs.

That highlights one significant issue. Some entrepreneurs work on the *craft of writing a proposal* rather than on the *value of the content*. Being a great "writer" in terms of grammar and technique is wonderful but not likely to create a compelling story for you. Popular authors like John Maxwell, Seth Godin, Chris Brogan, and Jim Collins are not known for their mastery of the English language, but for the focused content they present. The same principle applies when writing a compelling sponsorship proposal.

Do I need to write a sponsorship proposal?

There are many reasons entrepreneurs need to write a sponsorship proposal. The choice is up to you. Your motivations are probably a combination of these factors:

- **Communication:** Creating a sponsorship proposal is a wonderful way to communicate your message to a broader audience. If you are a speaker or educator you can exponentially increase your audience. If you have any area of expertise, engaging corporate sponsorships help you leverage that expertise. Creating a sponsorship proposal will help you find your own voice. It will help you trust that you have something important to offer. You have a product or service that must be communicated. I didn't start out wanting to create high impact sponsorship proposals—I started by struggling with people who were trying to find meaning in their work and wanted to share those principles with more people.

- **Fame**: Yes, there is a certain amount of celebrity status that comes instantly when receiving a sponsorship gift. Many entrepreneurs, speakers, nonprofit leaders, authors, associations, board of directors, event planners, entertainers, journalists, sports, political, and media figures are receiving sponsorship dollars. A sponsorship says that you have moved up the ladder significantly. A sponsorship crevates sustainability and in some cases creates a legacy of thought and insight that will hopefully continue long after you are gone. It's a thrill to run into someone in an airport, on a cruise ship, or at the mall who has heard of your work and say I want to be just like you.

- **Fortune**: Okay, we certainly hear about the famous 'ones'— Steve Jobs, John Greshams, Ray Kroc and Henry Fords of the world—where other peoples money helped to make them millionaires over and over. But recognize how extremely rare that is. It does happen, but the odds are stacked against you. There are lots of ways to make money more easily than hoping it will come from a sponsorship—but keep planning for it to happen to you.

- **Credibility**: Receiving a sponsorship helps to position you as an expert in your field. It's like writing a book. If you are a consultant, speaker, coach, pastor, or nonprofit executive, receiving a corporate sponsorship is a valuable gift for establishing your credibility as a person who is an expert. It has been said there are two ways to document your credibility.

Ω Get a Ph.D

Ω Writing a book—writing a book will force you to grow intellectually by reading more, researching more and then assimilating that information into a format that can be easily understood by your reader.

Now turn the same philosophies of writing a book into writing a compelling sponsorship proposal.

I tend to view my sponsorship proposals as powerful business cards for drawing customers into the different aspects of my brand. Corporations, who support your business through sponsorships may then purchase your products, attend seminars and workshops, and request personal coaching. If you view your brand as the end product and put all your hopes on garnering sponsorship dollars, you may be disappointed—but if you position it as one part of your larger business, it can be a vital component of your larger success. Every sponsorship request should promote and help sell each of the products and services you offer. If done properly, your sponsorship proposal creates a sales funnel, leading to speaking, consulting, eBooks, audio products, and workshops.

Before you begin

I encourage you to approach your sponsorship writing as a business proposal. Too often authors will write a book like many artists paint a picture, just hoping that it will get noticed or that someone will agree to the sponsorship opportunity. Your strategy must be more strategic about the process. You are about to invest a significant amount of time and energy; thus, it's reasonable to ask yourself these ten questions:

- Does creating a sponsorship align with my purpose?
- Will it be an expression of my passion?

- What is the purpose of the proposal? Why do I feel compelled to write it?
- Who am I writing the proposal for?
- What are the characteristics of the partner who will definitely want to support me? Each proposal must be personalized— we will talk more about personalization in a later chapter.
- Do I have the skills to turn my passion into meaningful work?
- Why am I so eager to use this format to secure funding?
- Has my message been written? What is remarkable about your value?
- Am I committed to spending time researching potential partners? Passion and talent are fine, but by themselves do not necessarily generate income.
- How does securing sponsorships fit into my overall mission, business, and career?
- If I have a plan, what's stopping me from starting today?

What are the steps to captivating a business partner?
Create a wish list of sponsors, consider

- What products and services does your target audience use?
- What social connections do you have to offer a sponsor?
- Who sponsors organizations similar to yours?
- Who are their competitors?
- Research your demographics.
- Get to know and understand your target audience.
- Among your competitors, who is successful with their sponsorship programs?
- Review websites, social media outlets, journals, magazines, TV, etc.

- Keep a notepad handy to write down names of companies until you find a niche…begin with 50 corporations. You can always change and modify the list.

Research each of your sponsors

- Review their company website in great detail. You will learn valuable information to add to your proposal.
- Social media profiles. Most companies and their staff will have social media profiles. You can discover whom you need to speak to and offers you networking opportunities.
- Make use of Google search to look for references to a company's brand. You may want to limit to your geographical area and use the Google Advanced Search to limit the results to the last 12 months. Example keywords…
  - Sponsor/sponsorship
  - Market/marketing/marketing plan/marketing strategy
  - Target audience/target market
  - Annual report for publicly listed companies
- Create Google alerts to keep up-to-date with the latest news on a potential sponsor. These are automatic emails sent to you when Google finds relevant information about a potential sponsor.
- Hoovers.com is an alternative to finding valuable information about a potential sponsor.

Create a research template to document your findings. A sample is provided in the tools section.
Template Includes

- Company Name
- Location

- Compatibility score—we'll discuss in a bit
- Primary and secondary contact information
- Website and social media links
- A list of brands, products, and services
- The sponsor's marketing objectives
- Target audience details
- Current sponsorship arrangements—a list of existing sponsorships
- Operational areas and geography
- General notes
- Communications log—used to track the who, what, when, and how of your interactions with the sponsor

Before contacting a potential sponsor, do a reality check using a Sponsor Compatibility Matrix. At this point the research should give you a pretty clear picture of the opportunities **not** worth pursuing. Reasons will vary, which could include non-compatible niche, company policies, etc.

I found this matrix online; it's not my original work. However, I use this as my guide when rating potential sponsors. You can quickly see the opportunities that are ahead for you. First, using the Sponsor Compatibility Matrix, calculate the compatibility score.

"The matrix includes 8 attributes you rate from 1 to 10; the higher the score the better the compatibility" (Skildum-Reid, K. and Grey, A., 2010)

8 Compatibility Attributes

1. Relationships—do you have an existing relationship or connection with the sponsor?

2. Objectives—Do you fit with the marketing objectives of the sponsor?

3. Audience—How closely do you share a common target audience?

4. Competition—Does their competition use sponsorship in your areas as a marketing tool?

5. Attributes—How closely do the attributes of what you have to offer match or compliment that of the sponsor? E.g. sophisticated, smart, loud, family oriented, original.

6. Geography—Does the sponsor operate in the same geography as you have marketing objectives targeting the same level? E.g. National, state, region, city, district, suburb.

7. Comfort—How comfortable are they using sponsorship as a marketing tool? Do they have a strong sponsorship history?

8. Size—How big is the sponsor compared to the value you can provide? The bigger the gap the less compatibility. E.g. Sony is unlikely to sponsor the local junior soccer team.

Now that you completed the matrix you can see where your research will help you determine what numbers feel right. Ranking your potential sponsors will be easy to place in order of compatibility; the higher the score the better your chances. Sample telephone scripts can be found in tools.

Pick up the phone and contact your hot list of sponsors. Here is the hard part for many people, calling a potential sponsor. What do I say? Not to worry, we provide samples for you to customize for your use. Use your hot list from the compatibility matrix, pick up the phone and start calling. You know your passion—you're ready to tell someone else. It needs to come from your own words, feelings, and emotions.

How do I sell a first-time sponsorship?

As promised earlier in this section, how do you sell a first-time sponsorship?

- Fill your offerings bag with your assets and related benefits
- Seek out a media partner, this will add great value to your benefits
- Cultivate strategic alliances with businesses and public organizations that have a strong track record of success
- Create an advisory board of influential people that will become your cheerleader
- Research…research…research. You can never do too much research on the corporations you plan to submit your proposal
- Develop your short-term and long-term marketing plan
- Be clear and realistic about your demographics and extended networking reach
- Consider working with an in-kind sponsor or trade to allow you to increase your value to potential sponsors

BONUS

To learn specifics about a corporation, go to their company website or www.Hoover.com and look for their strategic plan and/or annual report. You will uncover valuable information for your sponsorship proposal.

What do business partners look for?

You may be interested to know what sponsors are looking for. Many have a long history of supporting the public sector and entrepreneurs. So even if you are a marketing whiz you will want to be familiar with all the ins and outs of writing a compelling proposal.

First, be aware that 90% of sponsorship proposals go directly to the marketing executives. Most will have a set of standards and guidelines to follow when making a decision to support or not support your property. From my research marketers will reject nearly 99% of first-time proposals they receive. Of course they look for compelling stories and organizations that are in alignment with their mission and strategic goals for supporting the community and increasing their bottom line. If you're looking for the standard sponsorship proposal, you've come to the wrong place. Each proposal needs to be customized to meet the needs of the sponsor.

Ultimately sponsors are looking for three specific things:

1. A compelling story—this is a given. The message must be fresh and offer a new perspective. There must be a market need and a "hook" to engage the sponsor. While there must be a new element to your property, NEVER tell the decision maker there is "nothing like this" that's ever been done before. That will get you rejected quickly.

2. Clear Premise—do you have a clear premise? Have you identified a need and proposed solution? Have you stated that clearly in 2-3 sentences? A lengthy or unclear premise will tell the decision maker instantly that the proposal will be unclear as well. Think of it this way—a sponsorship proposal is a pre-packaged solution to a problem. Get used to getting to the point quickly. In many proposals writers will spend far too much time telling the sponsor what they are going to talk about.

3. Marketing and reach—this is expected in a proposal. How will you market your sponsor to your client's, network, media etc.? You need to be exceptionally creative when listing your marketing benefits.

No matter how wonderful your knowledge of the content presented, no one will know about you or your property unless you promote and market your work. I have been researching 'how to write' compelling proposals through conversations with corporate decision makers. The most important takeaway I will share is that 90 percent of your success comes from your ability to promote and market your sponsor.

Recognize that there are plenty of wonderful proposals submitted to corporations everyday. Your proposal may represent thousands of hours of research, and take months before you receive a response. What I am telling you is not to put all your resources in one basket. You need to diversify by creating exceptional income by using your property to drive traffic back to your website where you provide a variety of products and services for a cost. Don't sit quietly while hoping for a major sponsor to solve your financial needs.

Writing a compelling sponsorship proposal requires organization and discipline. You must approach it just as you would an ice cream truck business or planning an event. Don't expect a magical moment of inspiration that causes something great to appear. No, I find that great proposals come from productive people. Set aside large blocks of time for creating, whether you feel inspired or not. Practice by writing blogs or newsletters; be intentional. I am intentional with my Monday morning blog posts. This is not always my most inspirational time of the day or week, but I know it's on my calendar as my creative writing time. Once I start researching a topic I type words that come to mind, later the inspiration kicks in and I am able to go back and rewrite with a more compelling story.

BONUS

Keep note pads everywhere—next to your bed, in your car, on the refrigerator, and in the bathroom. When you have a thought about something that would add to the proposal—write it down before you forget. Of course if you're driving you may prefer to use your voice memo on your cell. Most people will lose their best ideas because they say "I'll remember" then lose the thought when they are back to writing their proposal. Become skillful in capturing useful ideas that enter your mind. They will come to you at the most inopportune times.

How do I know which corporation would be interested in becoming my business partner?

Discovery Interview

Hello, may I speak to John? (Marketing department, public relations, community relations, etc. You will need to research the appropriate contact.) This is Connie from *Get to Work*. We're interviewing potential business partners. Do you handle the corporate sponsors?

[Sample Questions}

- Are you interested in cause-related marketing?
- Can you provide me a sample of your sponsorship guidelines?
- Would you be interested in generating more revenue?
- Do you want to connect Women Executives and create a brand friendly environment?
- [let the interviewee know you are a nonprofit and/or have a partnership with a charity, and their gift is possibly a tax-deduction]

As a business partner you will receive the usual marketing campaign—tell me, what would your business want included in a sponsorship package?

- A featured article in the Association Newsletter (circulation 270,000 Quarterly)
- Ad in the event program book
- Signage at the event
- Marketing in the Association promotional material pre and post event
- Banner ad on the Association website

I have a brief proposal that I will personalize for you. I'd also like to verify your business address, telephone number and fax? Do you have an email address? [I suggest you have a separate work sheet available to receive the updated contact information.]

Closing

It's been great talking with you today. Do you recommend anyone else that would be a potential sponsor? Thank you for your time and consideration.

TELEPHONE CONFIRMATION SHEET

Today's Date: _____/ _____/ _____

Name of Contact: _____

Business Name: _____

Address of Business: _____

City/State/Zip: _____

Main Phone Number: _____

Best Time to Call: _____

Contact Direct Phone Number: _____

Contact Email: _____

Date proposal mailed: _____ / _____ / _____

Date discovery questions Emailed: _____ / _____ / _____

Additional Comments: _____

_____

Date entered into database: _____ / _____ / _____

Follow up Schedule: _____ / _____ / _____

Basic Telephone Scripts

One of the greatest fears I encounter is telephone "brain freeze." When I was working with the United States Chamber of Commerce, one of the telemarketers had a fear of talking on the telephone. In person, he could sell you anything. Put a telephone in his hands, and he froze.

An exercise to help him overcome his fear of the telephone was to set an egg timer in front of him. He had exactly the time of the egg timer to get his point across to the person on the other end of the line. The timer started at "Hello." Do you know anyone like this?

Whether you have a fear of the telephone or speaking to a potential customer face-to-face, be prepared. When you are prepared you will have greater confidence in yourself. If you are not prepared, it will show up in your conversation. One way to be prepared before picking up the telephone is to create a telephone script. The following pages provide sample scripts to use as a guide. The scripts may be changed to fit your needs and the mission of your organization.

One trick I learned from my coach is when you ask a question, wait for the answer. STOP TALKING. This will take a bit of practice, because 30 seconds may seem more like 30 hours, and the first one to speak loses. If the potential customer starts to ask questions back, you're in!

What is the best way to approach a potential customer?

- Be sure you talk to the decision maker.
- Speak effectively; make notes of their objections and concerns. Listen for any "hidden message."
- Ask for their decision maker (use a real name), and then be quiet. This is extremely important. I'll refer to this technique many times throughout the following pages.

Expo Participation Commitment

Hello. I'm Connie of *Get to Work*, which, as you no doubt know is the largest learning center providing educational services and opportunities for our clients.

We will be holding a job expo on April 25: to be held at the local hotel and convention center. The event will be running from 12:30 to 5:00 pm.

We will feature a "Dress for Success" fashion show to include apparel for men and women, resume writing workshops, booth exhibits, contests, and giveaways for the attendees.

We expect approximately 1,200 attendees. You were suggested, and we also feel that you are a perfect match as the top sponsor of the event.

BENEFITS

- This will get you in front of your audience.
- Exposure to over 1,200 attendees.
- You will be the only top sponsor of the event. (Provide details of sponsor benefits you are offering?)
- Many more benefits too numerous to mention over the telephone.

The reason for my call today is that I can be available as early as (day) to stop by and discuss in more detail with you! Would you like to meet in the morning or afternoon?

**SPEAK WITH ENTHUSIASM!
IT'S CONTAGEOUS!**

Getting Through the Gatekeeper

Hello. I'm Connie Pheiff, and I am calling to speak to the president/owner/decision-maker of [business name.] Is he or she in? Tell him or her I'm calling about a business proposal and would like to speak to him or her.

You have several options here. Some may sound simple, but they work. I know because I have tested and used these techniques over and over again.

- Get to know the gatekeeper.
- Set up a meeting with the decision maker.
- Ask the gatekeeper for help if the decision maker is not available.
- Ask when the decision maker will be available
- Start a conversation with the gatekeeper; ask open-ended questions, such as when will the decision maker be available? I am in the area often. If I see the decision maker's car, I will stop by. Ask what type of car the decision maker drives.
- Don't be afraid to ask questions.
- Don't be in a hurry to tell who you are or why you are calling. Keep the gatekeeper intrigued.

Getting the Meeting with the Decision Maker

Hello. I'm Connie of *Get to Work*, which, as you no doubt know is the largest learning center providing educational services and opportunities for our clients.

The organization has been in existence since 1984. Since that time our services have been increasing to include expanded global. Our services have grown to include career seminars for both men and women. While our services are increasing, so are customer needs. With help from business leaders such as you, we have been able to increase services in most cases.

Since the beginning we recognized one basic fact: every case, every individual is different. This is why we have no set plan or preconceived ideas about how your business can help. That is why I am here: to show you how supporting the mission of *Get to Work* will have a positive impact on your business, what you should know about us, and how your support will gain additional business in the next year.

Do you have a marketing budget? If you don't have a marketing plan, we can create one for you. To achieve this, we have various ways you can partner with us.

Now, so that I can more intelligently talk about how we can work together, I would like to ask you a couple of questions. (Use two or three questions; too many will end the conversation. The goal is to get the decision maker talking about his or her passion for giving.)

- What has been your marketing goal in the past year? What were the most important results you?
- What are your biggest opportunities you want to take advantage of?
- What are the biggest challenges you are facing?

- What measurements will tell your strategies for marketing are highly successful and meaningful to your business?
- What would it cost you if you failed your objective?

Because of economic conditions and competition, we know that today every business has concerns about where they spend their dollars. What do you consider to be your three main business concerns?

Training the right people for your business is what we do best at *Get to Work*. Here is how we can help solve your problem (Provide samples of your organizations newsletters, email blasts, website, or events where the company receives immediate marketing opportunities. This "creative marketing," add this technique to your system.)

We look forward to developing a great working relationship. When do you want to get started?

"I need time to consider."

Perfect, how much time do you need?

STOP AND BE QUIET. Let the customer speak first.

You can use the following telephone script during campaign season, if you are an organization with a concern about the election results. This is one I used when working with the United States Chamber of Commerce.

Election Pitch

It probably goes without saying that we are very concerned about the November elections. We think they are going to be critically important for small business. The Chamber's Board has me getting in touch with each of our members. To be blunt, we need some help. Do you have a moment to talk about it?

We have a razor thin majority in both the House and Senate. Loss of just a few seats means the chairman of the Senate Labor and Human Resources Committee, and speaker of the House and other possibilities too scary to mention.

On the other side of the coin, if we can gain a few seats, we can override vetoes coming out of the White House, and all of a sudden we have a chance to do something real about the liability problem, over-regulation, taxes, and so forth. It would certainly make living with the final two years of the current administration much easier to deal with.

We cannot allow a coalition of unions, trial lawyers, and radical environmentalists to buy the next election. The AFL-CIO alone spent more than 35 million dollars, and they have committed almost twice as much for next year. Who knows how much the trial lawyers have set aside to make sure their gravy train doesn't disappear.

The Chamber is working nationwide to identify races that can go either way and that have a clear cut philosophical difference between the candidates. We are then doing everything we can to get the folks with the white hats back here to Washington where they can do some good.

The problem is simple. If we are going to do this right, it is going to be expensive. The Chamber's Board is asking each of our members to help in underwriting the cost. One nice thing about it is that your contribution is tax deductible in the same way that your dues are. This is not a PAC; we do not give money to candidates or parties. Most of our members are kicking in an amount equal to their current dues. I'm on the phone to make sure we can count on the help from the Smith Company.

Are you in? **STOP AND BE QUIET**. Let the customer speak first.

What is the best approach to the "ask?"

I find the best approach to the "ask" is a direct hit. Whether you are going for a customer of a Fortune 100 company CEO's or a local mom and pop business, the best approach is not to waste anyone's time. We are all busy. We are doing more with less. When I call to schedule an appointment, I let the decision maker know why I am coming. When you tell the decision maker where you are calling from and why, they will know immediately why you are calling. The conversation often turns into your making your pitch over the telephone. I would recommend not making a 'cold' call. They're painful. Rather prep this potential customer through service.

Be open, direct, and touch your customers frequently!

Membership Letters

Earlier I mentioned the loss of the Chamber health care benefit. Entrepreneurs need assistance from organizations such as the Chamber of Commerce group association to create a program that will offset the cost of coverage. The loss of this benefit was costly to the Chamber in terms of membership loss and dollars. In the weeks and months to follow, a coalition of Chamber organizations teamed up to research and create a new program.

After nearly one year to the date, a new program was launched. Unfortunately, that came too late for many of the members who could not wait for the Chamber to get their ducks in a row. It was my job to regain the membership loss. This took some creative marketing. I started with telephone calls to ask members to rejoin and to ask local businesses to become a Chamber member for the first time.

The first program developed was the Chamber's Ambassador Committee. I was able to increase the 6-person committee to 86 in one year. If you are a membership organization, yes entrepreneurs have memberships; the following letters will be a helpful source of information.

Invitation to Join
Simple Version

Dear Jane,

Thank you for your interest in joining the Area Chamber of Commerce. Great things are happening at the Chamber lately. We led the way on saving jobs at a local manufacturing company; the region was named one of the 10 "All-American Cities" in 20xx based in part on the Chamber-managed Regional Economic Development Strategies, and we earned an "Equality Award" from the Urban League.

We continue to represent the business community on the local, state, and federal levels, assist our small and growing companies, and support education and workforce programs.

Our professional development programs, networking opportunities, and free consultation through our Business Solutions Center offer your business the best "return on investment" for your membership.

Please look over the materials in this packet and call me at 570.555.5555, if you have any questions. I look forward to welcoming you as the Chamber's newest member!

Sincerely,

Invitation to Join
Simple Version

Dear John,

The mission of the Chamber of Commerce is to help businesses flourish and prosper. Thank you for your inquiry regarding membership in the Chamber of Commerce. Your business and employees can benefit from Chamber membership in many ways, such as the following: [list your benefits, for example]

- *Discounted telephone long-distance services*
- *Group health insurance plans*
- *Valuable business contacts through networking opportunities*
- *Increased business skills for you and your employees by attending professional business seminars.*
- *Business referrals to you from the Chamber.*
- *Be in tune with local business issues that may affect your business by receiving the Chamber eNews Blast.*
- *FREE airtime with local media outlets (value $1,000)*

Business happens today. Don't wait to take advantage of these and other member-exclusive benefits! Join the Chamber today, and let us work for you.

Sincerely,

Invitation to Join
Long Version

Dear Jane,

Thank you for your interest in the State's Convention and Visitor's Bureau membership.

I have enclosed our membership package for your consideration. You are probably asking, "How will this membership benefit me and my business?" Honestly, many of our members were asking the same question before becoming a member of the bureau. I suggest looking at our website, contacting other bureau members, and taking a test ride by attending one, two, or three of our programs FREE.

You will learn about how our members benefit from membership. You will receive a FREE business listing on our website and publications.

After checking us out, if you still have questions about the benefits and services we offer, give me a call to schedule a personal visit to discuss membership.

The state is flourishing, and business is thriving, and this is the perfect time to join a membership organization where every member benefits.

Membership costs $_____ and is a one-year membership from the date you join. We accept all major credit cards, cash, and checks.

Like what you see? Complete the enclosed membership application, and return it to the bureau with your investment of $_____ made payable to the State's Convention and Visitor's Bureau, or call and we can bill your credit card and start your membership benefits today. We look forward to welcoming you and your organization as new bureau members!

Welcome,

Invitation to Join
Long Version

Dear John,

Thank you for your recent request for information on membership in the Chamber of Commerce. To help you make the best decision about participating in our association, I have enclosed some information about the Chamber's mission, plan of work, member services, and benefits.

You will discover that membership in the Chamber of Commerce is an investment in the future of our community and its economic development. As a Chamber member, you will also have the opportunity to help carry out the Chamber's program of work and give your business a great deal of positive exposure through networking, sponsorship, and marketing opportunities. And let's not forget about the Chamber benefits:

- *Discounted telephone long-distance services*
- *Group health insurance plans*

- *Valuable business contacts through networking opportunities*
- *Increased business skills for you and your employees by attending professional business seminars.*
- *Business referrals to you from the Chamber.*
- *Be in tune with local business issues that may affect your business by receiving the Chamber's eNews Blast.*
- *FREE airtime with local media outlets (value $1,000)*

The Chamber's staff and volunteer ambassadors are committed to working hard on your behalf to insure the future of the local economy and quality of life. It is important to be part of a group that takes this kind of initiative to make a difference.

After taking a few minutes to review the enclosed information, John, I am confident you will like what you see. If you have any questions, please do not hesitate to call me at the Chamber office, 570.555.5555.

*Personality can open doors—
but only character can keep them open.*
—Elmer G. Letterman

Telephone Scripts

I have had several mentors or coaches in my life. At the time, I didn't think of these people as coaches or mentors, but looking back now, I see that they really were.

No matter where you are in your professional career, don't be afraid to seek out a coach.[2] Look for somebody who is a successful entrepreneur, a person you admire or would want to emulate. You could also seek out

---

2   You can get more information about *Green Apples Impact Academy* and one-on-one coaching with Connie Pheiff by completing a contact form found at www.conniepheiffspeaks.com or send an email to TEAMPHEIFF@conniepheiffspeaks.com.

a professional coach, someone to whom you pay a fee for their coaching services. Either way, it'll be an investment in yourself you'll never regret.

I quickly learned from my coach *The Art of the "Ask."* Good communication is important when speaking to a customer in person, through a letter, or over the telephone. A conversation over the telephone is as important as having a face-to-face conversation. The person on the other end can "read" your body language, knows if you are passionate about your work, and appreciates your candor and integrity.

Invitation to Join
National Member Track

Hi, John. This is Connie. Thank you for taking my call. I'm calling from the National Association. I'm calling quickly; —first to update you on our nationwide campaign to pass our business legislative program; second, to ask for your support of our work on behalf of small business. Vital legislation is up for a vote in congress and will have a major impact on business.

You may have been reading about this campaign already. There are a dozen new bills designed to help small business stay profitable and competitive. It's the most important legislation in the last ten years.

The three most crucial bills are legal reform, regulatory relief, and a small business tax package. Our most important goal is to pass liability reform this year.

We have declared war on trial lawyers. We're fighting to level the playing field and end lawsuit abuse against business. Don't you agree we have to get this done?

Senate Bill 555, the Liability Reform Act, features caps on punitive damages and fair share liability. It also specifically protects small businesses with fewer than 25 employees.

We need your support as a member. Our dues are $_____. Can we count on you, too?

WAIT. WAIT FOR AN ANSWER.

Great. I'll send a statement for $_____ to your attention. Or I could save you time and a stamp by putting your dues on a credit card. Thank you.

Invitation to Join/Renew
National Member Track

Hi, John. This is Connie. Thank you for taking my call. I'm calling from the National Association. I'm calling quickly. Our Board of Directors has asked me to alert the business community, through our membership, to legislation that will cause a dramatic increase to the overall net profit of all businesses. It's important, and it'll only take a couple of minutes, if you have the time. Great!

- Liability reform
- Regulation reform
- Income tax reform

All are poised for action in Congress.

To make this pending legislation law, we must elect a pro-business Congress. Right now, we have a Republican majority, not a pro-business one. Even though this congress is sympathetic to business interest, they are not passionate about your needs.

In the last election, there was a net loss of 145 representatives, because the head of the unions spent $35M to buy a Congress. (Pause) Right now the unions have $60M stashed away because of the new credit cards the union has issued. Their "war chest" for the upcoming election is twice as big, because they got an additional $12M from raising all union dues nationally.

Let's say he only does as well as he did in the last election. We lose the Republican majority in Congress, kiss the recently won tax relief good bye, and forget about liability, regulation, and income tax reform.

I don't know whether you're aware that the organization has a new president. The first order of business is to serve notice that we will not allow the unions to buy through legislation what they cannot negotiate at the bargaining tables.

John, to elect a pro-business Congress, we must have the financial involvement of business now. By investing $_____ to $_____, it not only gives us the necessary resources to continue shrinking the federal government; it also gives us the opportunity to meet the challenges and elect a Congress favorable to your needs.

The response has been great! Ex: 80% committed $_____, 45% for the full amount. Let's cut to the chase: we need your commitment now. May we count on you, too?

WAIT. WAIT FOR AN ANSWER.

When one door of happiness closes, another opens, but often we look so long at the closed door that we do not see the one, which has been opened for us.
—Helen Keller

Membership
Renewal Track

Hi, Jane. This is Connie from the National Association. How are you today? Could I have a few minutes of your time to introduce myself to you as your new contact and to thank you for your past support of the National Association?

I also want to inform you that the United States Senate will be going to vote shortly on the product liability and legal reform Act of 2002. That's the bill that would put a cap on punitive damages for frivolous lawsuits. I want to get your opinion on the issues.

I am sure you're aware of the little old lady leaving a restaurant and splashing hot coffee on herself. Well, most people do not realize that their skyrocketing premiums are going to pay those legal fees. We really need to tame the lawsuit abuse in this country. We are fighting the trial lawyers' association on suits like this. We feel that the legal system is out of control. It is costing businesses and consumers billions of dollars per year. This has to change.

Your membership is up for renewal shortly, and we are asking our members to reinvest with us at this critical time to make sure our voice is heard. Then we can lobby with Congress to really cut this ridiculous spending and put some of the dollars where it is needed most: in your pocket.

Last year your total investment was $_____. Can we count on $_____ investment this year?

WAIT FOR IT!

Membership
Renewal Track

Hi, Jane. This is Connie from the local Chamber of Commerce. I see you have not renewed your annual membership.

After several months of invoicing and attempting to contact you, we have come to the conclusion that you do not wish to renew your membership. We sincerely hope you will reconsider your membership with the local Chamber of Commerce.

We count on local business to provide the community with support and feedback on important issues that businesses face each day. We offer excellent business opportunities through various programs, such as educational, environmental, small business loans, and awesome networking programs sponsored by businesses such as yours.

[Ask Questions]

- Let me ask, how many educational seminars will you pay to attend this year?

- How would you like to attend a Chamber seminar FREE?
- Did you know the Chamber offers free seminars? The topics range from labor law, business plan design, to securing an SBA loan.
- Why is the membership investment a concern?
- Why don't you consider using one of our three payment plans?

Don't let a business-building opportunity pass you by. Reinstate your Chamber membership today. Don't hesitate; reinstate your Chamber membership today.

Personal Touch

A good entrepreneur tells everyone about their business. That means you have to approach customers, both current and future, and consistently provide information about your business. Even if someone is a loyal customer and purchased your products | services every year for the past decade, you need to keep the conversation going about your and how your customer benefits.

Most people you'll be contacting have either shown an interest in your business previously, or they have made small purchases. Therefore, you're technically dealing with warm contacts rather than cold ones. That alone should ease any fears, increase your confidence, and help you become a *Marketing Master*.

What's the best way to get information to customers?

Many entrepreneurs think they need a glitzy brochure and other sales materials to present to customers. In reality, your customer doesn't want to see that, they want to know how you will serve them; solve their problem. I'm guilty of paying an advertiser lots of $$$ to create and print flyers that go out of date the day its was printed. Don't waste your money. Create a media kit and print on demand. Better yet, promote yourself by providing a service using your social networking sites. The information you provide will be relevant to your current business model. The same goes for any other media outlets where you may advertise, including billboards, radio and television ads, etc.

Additionally, if you're mailing that brochure or sales material, you have to pay for the postage. That alone can add up to a lot. Social media is a low-cost marketing option, but remember to research your market. If you work with baby boomers, many may have not embraced social networking as readily. If you rely primarily on social media to get your information out there, you're missing out on a large pool of potential customers. If you don't use social media, you're missing out on a large pool of potential customers. It's a double-edged sword.

When it comes to spreading your information, the best approach is to have multiple balls in the air. In other words, if you know someone wants to see a brochure, then send them one. If you know someone loves social media, then connect with them, like them, tweet with them, or Pin them. If you know someone prefers phone calls, then pick up the phone and call them. Do what each customer likes best. I still find the best approach is the old fashioned way: face-to-face.

Face-to-Face Presentation

Hello, Mr. Jones. I am Connie Pheiff from *Get to Work,* which, you no doubt know, is one of the largest learning centers providing services and employment opportunities for our clients. We've been around for nearly 50 years serving the general public, mostly people who have fallen on hard times. Due to economic conditions, there is a greater need for our services. We know that there is a need to broaden our reach to include neighboring counties. In most cases, we have been able to increase our services, but not completely. Funding the programs has become an issue. You understand?

Since opening our doors, we recognize one basic fact: every individual and his or her circumstances are different. This is the reason for my visit today. The need in our community is greater than ever before. We need your help.

Now, so that I can more intelligently talk about how we can help the community together, I would like to ask you a couple of questions. First, you have been a customer of ours in the past. What is your experience? What are your recommendations for increasing skills—skills to people who could possibly be your next employee? How can we make that happen?

Yes, I agree our business needs to increase community awareness of the issues. With that in mind can we count on your business again this year?

WAIT.

Thank you for your time and your honesty to help us serve our customers better.

How do I behave and have an impact with the customer when meeting face-to-face?

I find that when I meet with a customer, especially one of my larger customers, the discussion goes in the direction of the customer's needs. Let me set the stage here. Your business takes you into customer's homes. It's not your turf so how do you take charge of the conversation?

Greet your customer with a warm smile, a firm handshake, and a complimentary remark of some kind: "I love your décor," "You have an impressive business." Be honest with your compliment. If you are fake, the customer will feel it in your behavior. If you are offered something to drink, TAKE IT! If you decline a beverage, you are declining their hospitality, and they may decline making a purchase from you. I don't recommend drinking alcohol, unless the host is drinking a glass of wine. If so, then take it, sip it. Don't get sloshed.

Start off with a little small talk. Probe! The best topic is your customer. Learn more about his or her business, hobbies, and family. It's human nature; people like to talk about themselves. Look for a natural transition to the business at hand. One of the best conversation transitions is to ask the customer, "How is business?"

- Customer's will buy from people they know, like, and trust.
- Take control of the conversation to some extent. For example, suggest a place or seating arrangement for your meeting.
- Don't sit across from your potential donor. Sit beside them.
- Never give away your documents. You keep control of them and give them at the appropriate time, such as at the end of the meeting, as "leave-behinds."
- Make sure you are speaking with the decision maker. If there is a spouse or business partner who needs to be part of the decision, then you may want to reschedule to a time when you can meet with them together. Meeting individually is a time waster.

Close

The best close is a good opening. If you probed sufficiently to find out what motivates the customer, your presentation sold you. Your close is simply affirming the customer's commitment to work with you. The best closing attitude is to assume the customer commitment. In order to close the conversation, ask how the customer will provide the funds. Offer payment plans, if you have them.

Handle any questions or objections directly, and then keep going with the paperwork. The customer may ask, "Do I have to write a check today" Look the customer directly in the eye and say "yes" then, continue with your paperwork. Yes, a handshake is as good as gold, but I would have to say, "GET IT IN WRITING!"

We gain strength, courage, and confidence by each
experience in which we really stop to look fear in the
face…we must do that which we think we cannot.
—**Eleanor Roosevelt**

Is there such thing as writing a lengthy letter or Email?

Yes, did you ever receive a long marketing letter through mail or Email? How did you feel about the marketing approach? Did you read the entire letter? Can you tell me what's wrong with a lengthy letter? Put yourself in the shoes of a potential customer. What's wrong with this approach? It's too long; you lost me at hello. It's only natural to want to spill your guts, tell the customer everything about what you do, your products and services. But you never found out anything about this future customer. Let's be honest, though. Do you read every solicitation letter you receive? Another business is trying to sell me something. I would guess the answer is "no."

You best approach is simple social media ads, blogs, and stories about them. I do need to warn you, when you attempt to develop a 3x3 advertisement that says everything you offer—give me a call I would love to see your creation. Another option is creating a post-card. On the front of the postcard, list several bullets to communicate the benefits to your future customer and how you can solve their problem.

Volunteer your time to organize a charitable Event

Fundraising Telephone Track

Hello, may I speak to _____?

This is Connie, a volunteer for the local Chamber. I wanted to remind you about our summer cocktail party on the docks to be held on Friday, June 20, 20xx, from 6-8:30 pm. A presentation will be made to Representative Smith for his outstanding community leadership at about 6:45 pm. Will you be joining us? It's always a great time!

While I have you on the phone I would like to verify your work and home addresses and phone numbers? Do you have an email address?

Today a group of volunteers, including myself, are helping the Chamber with their Annual Appeal to raise $10,000. The funds will support youth programs and member activities. You should have recently received a letter describing the purpose of the Annual Appeal. Do you recall receiving this letter?

With membership dues covering only 60% of the program costs, the need for member support becomes increasingly important. We're asking each member to raise $500 for the Annual Appeal. I have made my commitment/pledge today and invite you to join me in the effort. Because the Chamber is a non-profit organization, your contribution is tax-deductible.

We have a special incentive this year. If your contribution is $50 or more and we receive your payment within ten days of this call, your name will be entered into a drawing for a $50 gift certificate to Bistro Bistro. There's even a second chance drawing. If we receive your payment within 30 days of this call, your name will be entered into a drawing for a $25 gift certificate to another area restaurant of your choice.

If previous donor—

Thank you for supporting us in the past.

If previous gift was $50 or more, ask for $100—

Can we count on your commitment or pledge of $100 at this time? (STOP! Don't speak until they do.)

If previous gift was less than $50, ask for $50—

Can we count on your commitment of $50 or more to help us reach our goal? (STOP! Don't speak until they do.)

If not a previous donor, ask for $50—

Can we count on your commitment of $50 or more to help us reach our goal? (STOP! Don't speak until they do.)

If asked what the money is used for—

Contributions are part of our operating budget and are used to maintain our professional, high quality programs. As a nonprofit organization, we need to keep programs affordable for small companies and individuals. These funds also support the scholarship fund, minority scholarships, and training materials for our youth.

If yes—

That's terrific (super, wonderful, etc.)! [Name], your pledge is really appreciated. We'll send you a note confirming your pledge with a return envelope. Remember to return your check within 20 days to be eligible for the drawing. Otherwise, we'll need to receive payment by the end of our fiscal year, June 30th. We are all proud to be part of the Chamber and hope you will continue to support it with both your time and money.

If undecided—

Is there another amount that would be better for you now?

If no—

May I send you a pledge card and a return envelope for your future consideration?

Closing—

It's been great talking to you. I also wanted to let you know that membership applications are available at the Chamber office. Please recommend a local business for Chamber membership.

Thank you for your consideration.

final thoughts

The teachings and stories in this book can be read from different perspectives from entrepreneurs to public and private corporate executives. I feel such richness when I write and share these tools with my friends—with you.

Stay Brilliant

The techniques and tactics provided will allow you to lead a successful business. I am confident once you start following the suggestions, your enterprise will begin to have customers calling you. In fact, I will guarantee it! Remember it takes risk to become great. You need to make up your mind, and it will happen. You will face many challenges as you change your "ways of work." You may experience setbacks, challenges, and failures. But don't let failure win. Brush yourself off, and start all over again. That's what it takes to create a system of creative marketing where you get Ready, Set, and GROW Your Market by developing creative marketing strategies to convert consumer's to a customers, relationships to partnerships, and ideas into realities. It's service, not sales that wins.

I wish you were here with me as I write my final thoughts and listening to Norman Greenbaum's *Spirit in the Sky*. When in doubt, listen to Norman and be a dancing fool!

Last year we moved to Southern California. I had never been in California until recently. We were packed by the moving company; fragile packages in the car with two dogs and mom and headed west. Mick Jagger, Stevie Nicks, Bob Dylan, and throw in a little Johnny Cash and Shania Twain to make the 5 $\frac{1}{2}$ day ride more bearable.

Before arriving in California I was already making contacts. People would laugh when I told them I was on my way to California and wanted to schedule time to talk about how I can serve. This was also posted to my social networks. The response was great, welcoming until the dreaded "…your work overlaps many other marketing consultants." Whew, my ego was bruised. But I held my head high and said, "You've never seen what I have to offer." I quickly got back on my horse and continued calling. I eventually confirmed a meeting with the Foundation Center that later scheduled an author event at each of their national locations—where I am the honored guest and keynote speaker.

My work is revolutionizing an industry. *Connie Pheiff Speaks, Marketing Masters Podcast, and Green Apples Impact Academy coaching* programs is a device for people serving people to feel good about them. When you can touch someone's heart, that's limitless.

When you learn to make small things unforgettable, understand and care about your customers, and have passion about what you're doing, you will !nnovate, Captivate, and Convert.

"Simple can be harder than complex. You have to work hard to get your thinking clean to make it simple. But it's worth it in the end, because once you get there, you can move mountains."

—Steve Jobs

acknowledgements

Academy award time—I will do my best to make it brief. In my previous book I included a dedication to my former employers thanking them for letting me go. As you can tell, the dedication was tongue-in-cheek, but it's true. If I were still working with these organizations, I might not have realized my skills and qualities to serve you.

Without these people in my life and supporting my work, I would not be here writing for you. I would like to thank

- My hubby Jeff who never complained about too many frozen dinners
- Barbara (Mom—well that story will be out in a novel)
- My business coach, Dan Miller, who keeps me focused on my vision

- My children, Stefanie & Michael
- My step-children, Jessica, Jeffrey, and Julie
- My dog who waits patiently to go pee when I'm writing
- My publisher, who made it all happen

recommended reading & resources

Here is my list of recommended books and resources for you to investigate. Most of the books listed can be purchased through my website, www.conniepheiffspeaks.com.

48 Days to the Work You Love: Preparing for the New Normal. — Dan Miller (2012)

Beyond Fundraising: New Strategies for Nonprofit Innovation and Investment. — Kay Sprinkel Grace (2010)

Crucial Confrontations: Tools for Resolving Broken Promises, Violated Expectations, and Bad Behavior. — Kerry Patterson, Joseph Grenny, Ron McMillan, and Al Switzler (2010)

Crucial Conversations: Tools for Talking When the Stakes are High. — Kerry Patterson, Joseph Grenny, Ron McMillan, and Al Switzler (2010)

Donor Centered Fundraising: How to Hold On to Your Donors and Raise Much More Money. — Penelope Burk (2007)

Marketing Pros (2014)

No More Mondays — Dan Miller (2010)

Reaching the Peak Performance Zone: How to Motivate Yourself and Others to Excel. — Gerald Kushel (2012)

Steve Jobs — Walter Isaacson (2013)

The 22 Immutable Laws of Marketing — Al Ries 7 Jack Trout (1994)

The Tipping Point: How Little Things Can Make a Big Difference. — Malcolm Gladwell (2011)

The Wisdom of the Flying Pig: Guidance and Inspiration for Managers and Leaders. — Jack Hayhow (2011)

Three Feet from Gold: Turn Your Obstacles into Opportunities. — Sharon L. Lechter, CPA, & Greg S. Reid (2009)

about the author

Connie Pheiff, best known as *Queen of the Ask*, is a former Director at the United States Chamber of Commerce and CEO of Girl Scouts. Connie is a professional speaker who brings style and substance to any event. She shares her powerful tools to help experts engage and release capacity for change.

In her internationally acclaimed **Green Apples Impact Academy**, Connie reveals her secrets to success sharing essential creative marketing and networking tools that will increase productivity, sales, and leadership, and propel you to the next level in your professional and personal life.

Whether you're an entrepreneur, an independent consultant, member of a sales team, development officer, or Fortune 500 CEO or somewhere in between, Connie will teach you innovative ways to start turning consumers to customers, relationships into partnerships, and ideas into realities.

She is CEO | President of the social media and content marketing consultancy group Connie Pheiff Speaks, Inc. A creative marketing pioneer, Connie has consulted with more than 700 entrepreneurs and corporations since 2006. She has worked with powerhouse organizations like UPS, United States Chamber of Commerce, American Red Cross, Dress for Success, Girl Scouts USA, and National Foundation Center.

The creator and host of *Marketing Masters*, a weekly radio show, which airs on Matrix Media, Inc. a Chicago-based radio syndication firm with credits, include Animal Planet Radio, Travel Channel Radio, The HGTV Design Minutes and the NBA Radio Network.

Looking for a dynamic keynote speaker for your next business meeting?
Call Connie Pheiff!

Looking for a visionary to revitalize your business?
Call Connie Pheiff!

Looking for a creative marketing and business coach to bolster your business?
Call Connie Pheiff!

How do you know what you want, when you have never seen it?
Call Connie Pheiff!

Would you like to be a guest on Marketing Masters?
Call Connie Pheiff!

"Connie's program was excellent. She hit it out of the park! She is soft-spoken, confident with a fierce grace, and delivers a message with a powerful punch."
[Recent program feedback]

Coach of multi-million dollar organizations, Connie's blog is ranked as one of the world's #1 for content and creative marketing strategies. When you're looking for a business and marketing coach, call Connie.

Connie's schedule fills up quickly each day. Her senior members of TEAM PHEIFF are accomplished speakers, workshop leaders, and coach who may be available to meet your training needs. Connie knows lots of great marketing speakers — even if Connie isn't available, contact TEAM PHEIFF for a customized and thoughtful referral.

Most Popular Keynotes | Workshops

- Creative Marketing: Ready, Set, GROW Your Market
- Get Your Groove Back to the Bank
- Social Networking: How Are You Connecting
- Molds are for Jell-O
- Streetwise Selling
- Executive Presence

Speaking Topics Include

- Creative Marketing
- Sales| Fundraising Strategies
- Digital Marketing
- Leadership
- Relationships

Many organizations ask Connie to deliver a seminar or breakout session in addition to her keynote.

To schedule Connie for a speaking engagement
email <u>TEAMPHEIFF@conniepheiffspeaks.com</u>
or call directly at 570.906.4395.

why book connie
for your next event

- Every presentation is customized to meet the client's needs
- Connie will use her reach to promote your event
- Visceral and visual. No boring PowerPoint presentation
- Connie is funny; attendees are guaranteed to leave laughing and thinking, and receive strategies they can immediately implement in their business
- Organized, on-time, considerate and easy to work with

Connie's goal is to be the best speaker and trainer you've worked with…ever! Event planners love working with Queen of the Ask, Connie! Call 570.906.4395 and book Connie today! TEAMPHEIFF@conniepheiffspeaks.com www.conniepheiffspeaks.com

Queen of the Ask

To be notified when additional books are published, please visit www.conniepheiffspeaks.com and sign up for Connie's newsletter and automatic alerts.

**Visit
www.conniepheiffspeaks.com for more information.**

Printed in the USA
CPSIA information can be obtained
at www.ICGtesting.com
JSHW022341140824
68134JS00019B/1612